FRANK LLOYD WRIGHT

AMERICAN ARCHITECT FOR THE TWENTIETH CENTURY

FRANK LLOYD WRIGHT

AMERICAN ARCHITECT FOR THE TWENTIETH CENTURY

ROBIN LANGLEY SOMMER

SMITHMARK

This edition published in 1993
by SMITHMARK Publishers Inc.,
16 East 32nd Street
New York, New York 10016.

SMITHMARK books are available for bulk purchase for sales promotion and premium use. For details write or telephone the Manager of Special Sales, SMITHMARK Publishers Inc., 16 East 32nd Street, New York, NY 10016. (212) 532-6600.

Produced by Brompton Books Corp.,
15 Sherwood Place,
Greenwich, CT 06830.

ISBN 0-8317-5160-6

Printed in Italy

10 9 8 7 6 5 4 3 2 1

PAGE 1: *The interior of the Susan Lawrence Dana House in Springfield, Illinois, contains furniture, art glass doors and windows designed by Wright, and a terra cotta fountain by sculptor Richard Bock.*

PAGE 2: *The Price Tower in Bartlesville, Oklahoma, built in 1953, was based on an earlier design, the 1929 St. Mark's Tower project in New York.*

Contents

Introduction

The early 1990s have seen a resurgence of interest in the architecture and decorative art of Frank Lloyd Wright (1867-1959) in conjunction with the 125th anniversary of his birth. More than ever, he is being recognized as a towering figure in the history of architecture and perhaps the greatest design influence in the United States during the first half of the twentieth century. Retrospective exhibits; new books by art historians, fellow architects, and people who studied and worked with Wright as members of the Taliesin Fellowship; commemorative lectures and papers; and, most recently, well-made and affordable reproductions licensed by the Frank Lloyd Wright Foundation, have all contributed to greater awareness of his life and work.

Many people who were aware of Wright's architectural landmarks, like the Edgar J. Kaufmann, Sr. House, Fallingwater, in Mill Run, Pennsylvania, have learned that he often designed everything connected with his projects, including furniture, art glass, lighting fixtures, table linens, carpets and carports (which he invented). It is now possible to own an object of Wright's design for far less than the 1.6 million dollars paid at auction for the original dining room set from the Joseph W. Husser House in Chicago, now demolished. Atelier International has reproduced designs for 30 pieces of furniture

from the Wright archives. Tiffany & Company offers china, crystal and silver vases, coffee services, and other objects of decorative art. The venerable textile-design house of F. Schumacher & Company has reissued the "Taliesin Line" of decorative fabrics and wallpapers that Wright designed in 1955, along with adaptations of his designs for rugs and fabrics.

Young American architects are among the foremost spokesmen for the enduring value of a Frank Lloyd Wright house. In fact, some of them have purchased a Wright house that had fallen upon hard

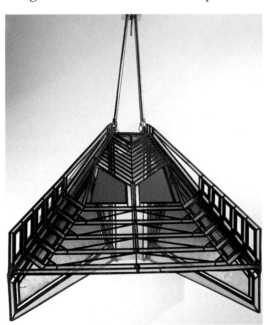

times and spent years restoring it. Philadelphia architect Albert H. Clark, and his wife Georgianna, purchased the former Sweeten House, built in 1950 in Cherry Hill, Pennsylvania. In a 1992 interview with Lucinda Fleeson of Knight-Ridder Newspapers, Clark said, "This house is more contemporary than most architects build today."

Since they purchased the single-story Usonian (from USONA, for United States of North America) in 1975, the Clarks have experienced both the enjoyment and the difficulties of owning an architectural legacy. Wright's Usonian houses were designed primarily for moderate-income American families, utilizing basic materials like concrete, glass, plywood and brick. Forty or fifty years later, it is often hard to match original construction materials for fidelity to Wright's designs and specifications. The mitered glass corners and window walls that unite the open, informal living areas inside with the outdoors also tend to bring in cold drafts in northern locations. Since Wright had a vehement aversion to screens, his clients had to order or build them themselves, as the Clarks have done. And the oversized fireplace that Wright considered the heart of the house, while a striking architectural feature, has the disadvantage of smoking when the fire dies down. Clark admitted that "We long ago sealed it. Now it's more a piece of sculpture." However, the heirs to Wright's legacy, like most of his clients throughout his 75-year career, consider these minor inconveniences as nothing compared to the pleasures of living in a work of art.

Wright's objectives in residential architecture remained remarkably constant, from his first designs as a draftsman with Adler & Sullivan in Chicago in 1888 to the end of his life. He envisioned the private home as a kind of citadel of family life, secure on its own property, centered around the hearth as the focal point for communal activities, with a free flow of interior space closely connected to the outdoors by porches, balconies and terraces. Unity, privacy and a sense of repose were achieved when every aspect of construction, furnishings and setting worked together in such a way that "The enclosed

Opposite above: A hanging lamp Frank Lloyd Wright designed for the Susan Lawrence Dana House, circa 1902.

Opposite below: Such Wright-designed features as furniture and carpeting integrate the interior of Taliesin North.

Below: The distinguished and innovative architect – Frank Lloyd Wright – at age 77.

Below: Wright designed this oversized fireplace for the Mrs. Clinton Walker House in 1948.

Right: This Carl Post residence typifies Wright's Usonian House design.

Opposite left: Wright's casement windows worked to unify interiors and exteriors. This window is in the B. Harley Bradley House (1900).

Opposite right: Bands of clerestory windows, designed for the Unity Temple in 1904, bring light into the sanctuary.

space itself might now be seen as the reality of the building." In *Two Lectures on Architecture*, published by the Art Institute of Chicago in 1931, Wright expanded on his definition of "organic architecture" when he stated that "This sense of interior space made exterior as architecture transcended all that had gone before. . . . The building now becomes a creation of interior space in light."

Wright extended these principles into all his most successful designs: commercial, ecclesiastical, educational, recreational, both executed and unbuilt. This was the principle underlying those diverse elements for which he became best known: soaring cantilevered balconies; broad, sheltering eaves; open floor plans; wooden valences that unify wall and ceiling; bands of clerestory windows and casements that open outward; structures that rise from their setting so naturally that it appears they have grown from the site rather than being constructed upon it. The workplace, the "good-time place," the house of worship, the home: all should enhance the dignity of the individual and permit his fullest realization as a member of his society. Wright's art was inseparable from his perception of the American cultural experience, both historic and ongoing, as reflected in such writings as *When Democracy Builds*. Jefferson, Emerson and Thoreau were part of the landscape of his

mind. The naturalism and individualism they professed, building blocks for the ideal "organic society," had a strong influence on him in concert with the Unitarian faith of his family, with its liberal and progressive philosophy. His Midwestern upbringing close to the land and the region's frontier heritage made an indelible mark. He said that "The real American spirit, capable of judging an issue for itself upon its merits, lies in the West and Middle West." It was no accident that fully two-thirds of the buildings he created in the course of his career were in the Middle West, incuding 43 in his native Wisconsin and 88 in his "adoptive" state of Illinois. The majority of his executed projects were houses, most of them in suburban settings.

Like his mentor Louis Sullivan, Wright maintained a cultivated aloofness from the city, which he perceived as dehumanizing in its congestion, pollution, and density of population. His Utopian ideas on city planning were expressed in *The Disappearing City*, published in 1932, and enlarged upon for the rest of his life in the Broadacre City projects that advocated decentralization and the union of modern technology with historical values for a more humane and enlightened society.

The man who would become this century's most influential architect was born in Richland Center, Wisconsin, on June 8, 1867. His father was William Cary Wright, a music teacher and Baptist minister who came from an English family of Nonconformists who had emigrated to New England early in the seventeenth century. Born in Westfield, Massachusetts, in 1825, William Wright studied law at Amherst College for a time, then chose the field of music and traveled widely as a teacher and preacher. He met his first wife, Permilia Holcomb, in Utica, New York,

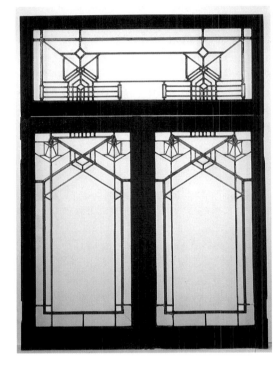

and they had four children.

The family finally settled in Lone Rock, Wisconsin, where they took in boarders to help make ends meet. One of these boarders was a teacher, Anna Lloyd Jones, the 27-year-old daughter of Welsh emigrants who had settled in rural Spring Green, Wisconsin. After Wright was widowed in 1864, Anna Lloyd Jones resolved to marry him, despite the 15-year difference in their ages and over the objections of her devoutly Unitarian family. The couple married in 1866, and Frank Lloyd Wright was born 10 months later. His sisters, Jane and Margaret Ellen (nicknamed Maginel) were born in 1869 and 1878, respectively. While William Wright's passion was music, his wife was passionate about education.

As Wright described in his autobiography, he was his mother's favorite from the beginning, and the bond between them became stronger as his parents' marriage

Frank was 18 years old, his parents separated and he entered the University of Wisconsin at Madison, where he worked for Allan D. Conover, a professor of engineering. (The first school of architecture in the country had opened at the Massachusetts Institute of Technology a year after his birth.) Apprenticed to Conover, Madison's only professional builder at the time, Wright also attended classes in the university's department of engineering for several years. In fact, this was his only formal training in drafting and the other technical skills of his future profession. His uncanny talent for drawing and the experience he acquired "on the job" in Conover's office were valuable assets when he left for Chicago early in 1887.

At that time, Chicago was experiencing an architectural renaissance in the wake of the great fire of 1871, which almost destroyed the city. One of the most sought-after designers was Joseph Lyman Silsbee, who had come from the East Coast to create a thriving practice, primarily in residential architecture, influenced by the work of Norman Shaw and his British contemporaries. Silsbee's "Shingle-style" houses were simple but elegant, and Midwesterners took him to their hearts. When

deteriorated. "The boy," as he called himself in *An Autobiography*, resembled his father physically and temperamentally, but his allegiance was to the Lloyd Jones side of the family. The Wrights lived for a time in Weymouth, Massachusetts, where Wright ministered to the small Baptist congregation and his wife pursued her educational interests. Frank Lloyd Wright stated that the family visited the Centennial Exposition in Philadelphia in 1876, and it was there that his mother learned about the progressive methods of education devised by the German educator Friedrich W. A. Froebel for children of preschool age. (It was Froebel who originated the term "kindergarten.") Mrs. Wright introduced her son to Froebel's system of games and "toys" that consisted mainly of simply shaped objects in primary colors – cubes, cylinders, squares and so forth. The child was encouraged to arrange these shapes into structures in various imaginative ways, and, as an adult, Wright claimed that his career in architecture was deeply influenced by this experience.

In 1877 the family moved back to Wisconsin, settling in Madison, the state capital, not far from Spring Green, where the children spent the summers at the farm of their uncle, James Lloyd Jones. When

Wright came to Chicago, Silsbee had recently been commissioned by Wright's uncle, the Reverend Jenkin Lloyd Jones, to design a new church for the congregation of All Souls' Church. Wright recalled that he had worked on the building, which had an informal asymmetrical design combining brickwork and shingles. It looked more like a house than a church, but the congregation was satisfied and used the building for several years, until it became too small for their needs.

Meanwhile, Wright had obtained a job as a draftsman with the highly regarded firm of Adler & Sullivan after seven or eight months in Chicago. Louis Sullivan (1856-1924), like Silsbee, was a transplanted Easterner. He had grown up in Boston, living mainly with his grandparents, who encouraged his love of nature and his interest in learning. At 16, he en-

rolled at the school of architecture at the Massachusetts Institute of Technology, where he stayed only a year before moving to Philadelphia. There he worked with architect Frank Furness, whose exuberant designs included the improbable Pennsylvania Academy of the Fine Arts, with its Gothic arches, elaborate friezes, columns and pediments. Sullivan then moved to Chicago, where he joined the staff of William Le Baron Jenney, one of the first architects of steel-framed buildings. Here he learned some of the ideas and techniques that would make him a master builder of the skyscraper, then emerging as the characteristic form of urban American architecture.

William Holabird and Martin Roche, then working with Jenney, who had studied engineering in Paris, at the École des Beaux-Arts, exposed the young Sulli-

van to European culture. Within a year, he departed for the Continent to resume his formal studies at the École des Beaux-Arts, the training ground for such eminent American architects of the day as New York City's Richard Morris Hunt and Henry Hobson Richardson.

After a short stay in Paris, Sullivan returned to Chicago and formed a partnership for the practice of architecture with Dankmar Adler, who concentrated on the business side of the firm. When Wright joined Adler & Sullivan, the partners had recently received the challenging commission for Chicago's Auditorium Building – a complex designed to contain a hotel, an office building, and an auditorium with a capacity of 4,200 people. Sullivan's innovative and successful design for the Auditorium Building of 1887-90, closely followed by such exceptional skyscrapers as the Wainwright Building in St. Louis, established him among the top rank of Chicago architects, led by Daniel H. Burnham and his brilliant young partner John Wellborn Root.

Wright, who called Sullivan "Leiber Meister" and deeply admired his 31-year-old mentor, rose rapidly in the firm. He was involved in the design for the great Neo-Romanesque Golden Door for the Transportation Building at the World's Columbian Exposition, held in Chicago in 1893. At the fair he was exposed to several influences that would have a lasting effect on his work: pre-Columbian architecture and Japanese culture, represented at the fair by a half-scale replica of a wooden temple from the Fujiwara period. Unlike most Midwesterners, Wright had already been exposed to Eastern culture by Silsbee, a collector of Orientalia. In time, he would become a notable collector himself, primarily of Japanese prints.

Within a few years of joining Adler & Sullivan, Wright met and married Catherine Lee Tobin, the daughter of a successful Chicago businessman. He had signed a five-year contract with Adler & Sullivan in 1889, which enabled him to build his own house in the suburb of Oak Park, next door to the house he had been sharing with his mother and two sisters. He and his bride took up residence there and Wright assumed all the responsibility for his firm's residential commissions in 1890. His earliest undertakings reflect what he had learned from Sullivan, whose work and ideas were a significant influence. As Manfredo Tafuri writes in *Modern Architecture*, published by Harry N. Abrams in 1976:

"Wholly original was Sullivan's capacity to reinterpret a model in his own terms and, above all, his astounding skill in integrating into his structures a naturalistic decorative vocabulary. . . . Sullivan viewed his efforts as part of a struggle for the restoration of the rights of the individual, of the subjective I as opposed to the mass, of the citizen, of democracy. . . . In the project for the Fraternity Temple in 1891, he attacked the problem of a global control of the total form of metropolitan centers and, in so doing, anticipated architectural types and problems characteristic of the twentieth century."

By 1893 draftsman Frank Lloyd Wright was attracting attention on his own merits. His designs were being commended by much older colleagues, and his ideas on arts and crafts as related to the machine age were quoted and debated. To meet the expenses of his rapidly growing family – the Wrights had five children in their first nine years of marriage, and a sixth later – Wright took on independent commissions for several clients in Oak Park, including houses for Walter and Thomas Gale. He called them his "bootlegged houses," although they did not directly violate his contract with Adler & Sullivan. He did the work on his own time, at night and over weekends, but when Sullivan learned of it in 1893, there was a heated quarrel and a breach that lasted for 20 years.

Wright opened his own office for the practice of architecture in Chicago, but by 1895 he had built his own studio adjacent to his house, in which he incorporated many of his ideas and tested them out, as he would in other home/studio settings all his life. It was here that he designed the first of his open-workspace plans, lighted from above by clerestory windows and furnished with pieces of his own design. Most of his work was being done in the Oak Park studio by the late 1890s, with the help of

Below: Wright's William H. Winslow House (1893) was a forerunner of his Prairie Houses.

Bottom: Wright gained national attention in 1901 with this design sketch, "A Home in a Prairie Town," published in *The Ladies' Home Journal*.

assistants who worked under his direction much as members of the Taliesin Fellowship would do in years to come. His office at Steinway Hall was used mainly for meetings with prospective clients and other business details. He shared the space with other young architects, including Dwight Perkins and Myron Hunt.

The 1890s saw a number of commissions that would become landmarks of Wright's early career. One of these was the 1893 design for the William H. Winslow House in River Forest, Illinois. From the beginning it was Wright's practice to supervise the construction of the houses he had designed, and many years later he told an amusing "on-site" story of the Winslow project. "I remember climbing up into an upper part of the building," he wrote, "to listen to comments. I pulled the ladder up and waited. In came a young fellow with a couple of young women and the fellow said, 'Have you seen the man who built

this? God, he looks as if he had a pain.' Another one said, 'They say this cost $30,000, but I can't see it.' I learned my lesson: I never listened like that again." (*New York Times* Magazine, Oct. 4, 1953).

The Winslow House, still remarkably well preserved, had a hip roof and wide eaves that made it a forerunner of the Prairie Houses that Wright would build, mainly in the suburbs of Chicago, during the early 1900s. He was working toward a style that would break away from the conventional boxlike dwelling, with its compartmentalized interior, toward the new architecture that he summed up in the phrase "Out of the ground and into the light!" He saw that an organic whole is not a fixed, final result, but essentially a process that is never really "finished." It is almost impossible to give the full effect of a Wright building in a photograph, or even in a model. Like a sculpture, it must be viewed from all sides, walked around,

"lived with" in a sense before it is fully appreciated.

Other important commissions of the 1890s included the Isidore Heller House in Chicago (1896) and the Joseph Husser House overlooking Lake Michigan. As Chicago expanded out into the surrounding countryside, the Husser House was encircled by new buildings that cut off its view of the lake. Eventually, it was demolished and lost to American architecture, except for a few photographs and the drawings in the archives of the Frank Lloyd Wright Foundation at Taliesin West, in Scottsdale, Arizona.

Wright's ideas first received national attention in 1901, when he contributed several model house designs to the Curtis Publishing Company for publication in *The Ladies' Home Journal*. The first was "A Home in a Prairie Town," designed to be built for about $7,000. Working drawings could be purchased by *Journal* readers at

five dollars per set. The attractive, horizontal house faced the street and had two tiers of shallow, broad-eaved hip roofs. The entry arch that Wright had been using since his days with Sullivan in one form or another was off-center, between the porte-cochere at one end of the house and a large covered porch at the other, adjacent to the living room. An alternative version provided for a two-story living room, which would become a Wright trademark, and the principal family rooms opened into another in an informal way.

The second design for *The Ladies' Home Journal*, "A Small House with Lots of Room in It," was budgeted at $5,800. The clearest executed example is the E. Arthur Davenport House in River Forest, Illinois, built in 1901 in collaboration with architect Webster Tomlinson. This is a two-story structure of stained-wood board and batten with plaster and a gabled roof. The front terrace has been removed, which fore-

Left: The E. Arthur Davenport House (1901) was executed using Wright's second design for *The Ladies' Home Journal*, "A Small House with Lots of Room in It."

Below: Wright's unexecuted design for sculptor Richard Bock's studio.

out of the second-story walls. Here was true enclosure of interior space."

In the same series of lectures, Wright explained the principles behind his treatment of ceiling space, which enhanced the human scale of his buildings. "The ceilings . . . could be brought over on to the walls, by way of the horizontal broad bands of plaster on the walls above the windows, the plaster colored the same as the room ceilings. This would bring the ceiling surface down to the very window tops. The ceilings thus expanded, by extending them downward," with the result that even small areas appeared larger and more spacious.

A decade of intense creativity began in 1900, with the first executed Prairie Houses, built for Harley Bradley and his brother-in-law Warren Hickox on adjacent lots in Kankakee, Illinois. Other commissions followed rapidly, to keep the small group at the Oak Park Studio working

shortens the appearance of the house, but its main features, including continuous bands of windows and the elimination of both attic and basement, are characteristic of the Prairie House. The gabled eaves are plastered, and the second story and cornice are defined by wood members.

A later design for the *Journal* was of a simple, square concrete house with a side entrance and a trellised terrace. The chimney supported the floors and carried the water from the roof. Summer ventilation was provided by square colored tiles beneath the eaves that could be opened and shut. Wright provided an alternate plan for placement on a given lot with each of these three designs – an example of the versatility that marked his innovative methods. In 1907 he would contribute a plan for a fireproof house at the request of the Curtis Publishing Company, which shared his interest in attractive, partly prefabricated houses available to the average family. Although most of Wright's clients at this time were wealthy suburban businessmen based in Chicago, he was always concerned with moderately priced housing for the average citizen, as reflected in several of his urban designs, including the Francisco Terrace Apartments (1895) in Chicago.

One of the most striking features of the Prairie House designs was the low cement or stone platform, resembling the stylobate of classical architecture, that replaced the customary foundation. Visually, they provided a line between house and site; structurally they carried the outside walls as far

as the second-story window sills. The upper level was generally treated as a gallery, often with an ornamental frieze in untreated natural materials like terracotta, with an overall foliage pattern in the style of Sullivan. The Winslow House is a striking example. As Wright explained it in the 1931 Kahn Lectures at Princeton University, published as *Modern Architecture* that same year by the Princeton University Press: "The rooms above come through in a continuous window series, under the broad eaves of a gently sloping over-hanging roof. This made enclosing screens out of the lower walls as well as light screens

almost around the clock. The first half of the decade saw the design and construction of the Ward W. Willet, William G. Fricke, Frank W. Thomas, Susan Lawrence Dana, William E. Martin, and Arthur Heurtley houses. Insofar as possible, Wright also designed the furniture and fittings for these houses, and collaborated with artists like George Niedecken, who painted murals for the Dana House and Wright's own home, and sculptor Richard Bock, who created the figures that ornamented the loggia of the Heller House and other projects, including the Oak Park Studio. The Luxfer Prism Company was

Below: The first executed Prairie House was the Warren Hickox House, built in 1900.

Bottom: The F. B. Henderson House (1911) features contrasting dark brown wood trim on white plaster.

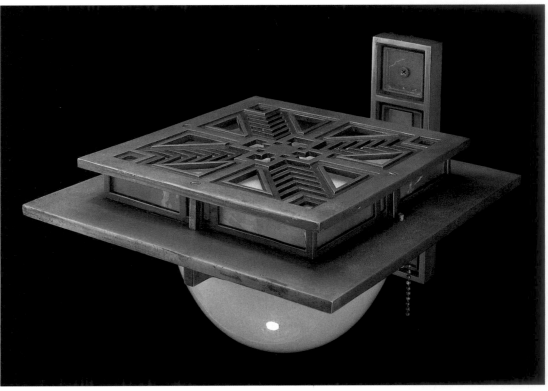

one of several companies with which Wright contracted for custom-made light fixtures.

The peak of Wright's Prairie House era came in 1906-07, with the houses created for Avery Coonley and Frederick C. Robie, the first in suburban Riverside, Illinois, and the second on a city lot in Chicago. In both cases, liberal clients with generous budgets gave Wright a free hand, and the results confirmed the fact that he had revolutionized residential architecture.

The Coonley House has a U-shaped plan using frame construction. Built over a raised basement, all its principal rooms except the children's playroom, at ground level, are on the second level, overlooking the lawns and garden from various heights. The horizontal lines of the house correspond to the interior plan, in which the space is arranged laterally to afford sweeping vistas unified by the spare, uncluttered design of Wright's built-in features and furnishings.

The Robie House, by contrast, is arranged along a single axis and built of brick and concrete, with projecting balconies and porches opening to the outdoors. There is no facade on the street side, no visible entrance, and no ornamentation, as such. The single most arresting feature of the exterior is the cantilevered roof that extends 20 feet beyond its masonry supports. Inside, the large central living space is defined, but not divided, by the chimney. This part of the house has no dividing walls or partitions – only a free flow of space richly embellished by burnished woodwork, patterned carpeting, art glass,

French doors, and the broad recessed hearth. Bedrooms, kitchen, and servants' quarters are set to the rear of the house.

The early 1900s also saw the construction of two public buildings that confounded the popular idea of what a church and a workplace should look like: Unity Temple, in Oak Park, and the Larkin Company Administration Building in Buffalo, New York. The poured-concrete monolith that Wright designed for Oak Park's Unitarian congregation in 1904, and the brooding brick mass of the Larkin Building, had their origins in Central Europe, according to Brendan Gill, author of the

brilliant biography *Many Masks: A Life of Frank Lloyd Wright*, published by G. P. Putnam's Sons in 1987. Gill writes: "Though Wright would have been quick to deny the truth of the assertion, the inspiration for the Larkin Building, and for Unity Temple had the same source: the Secession building in Vienna, designed by Joseph Maria Olbrich in 1898. Its function was to provide exhibition space for the art works of the so-called Secessionist *Kunst Haus* school, then commanding much attention throughout Europe and, to a lesser extent, in America as well. Olbrich was Wright's exact contemporary, having

Opposite above: The Frederick C. Robie House, completed in 1909, is a designated national landmark that preserves Wright's vision of the Prairie masonry structure.

Opposite below: Wright-designed light fixtures in the Avery Coonley House.

Below: Taliesin (1911) was built as a country retreat on Wright's mother's land in Spring Green, Wisconsin.

been born in 1867."

The first phase of Wright's career came to a close in 1909, when he was just over 40 years old. Leaving his wife and children behind, along with his practice, he departed for Europe with Mamah Borthwick Cheney, the wife of a client for whom he had designed a house in Oak Park some years before. The immediate occasion for his departure was an invitation from the German publisher Ernst Wasmuth to collaborate in producing a monograph of his works, *Ausgeführte Bauten und Entwurfe von Frank Lloyd Wright*. During an extended stay in Berlin and Florence, Wright completed the project, which was published in 1910. In his introduction to the Wasmuth portfolio, Wright did not lose his chance to take aim at the work of other architects – a lifelong practice that won him many enemies in his profession. He wrote: "I have called this feeling for the organic character of form and treatment the Gothic spirit, for it was more completely realized in the forms of that archi-

tecture, perhaps, than any other . . . the spirit in which they were conceived and wrought was one of absolute integrity of means to ends. In this spirit, America will find the forms best suited to her opportunities, her aims, and her life. The ideals of Ruskin and Morris and the teaching of the Beaux Arts have hitherto prevailed . . . New York is a tribute to the Beaux Arts so far as surface decoration goes, and underneath, a tribute to the American engineer."

When Wright and his companion returned from Europe in 1911, Mrs. Cheney was divorced and her husband received custody of their two children. She and Wright left the scandalized community of Oak Park behind and moved to what rural neighbors had long called "the valley of the God-Almighty Joneses" in Spring Green, Wisconsin. There Wright received a tract of hilly land from his mother, who had planned to build a cottage there in the wake of Wright's separation from his wife, Catherine, who was devastated by his desertion.

Wright went ever more deeply into debt in constructing the country retreat he called Taliesin – a Welsh name that means "shining brow." At first he planned to open a Chicago office, as well as the studio he was building in Spring Green, but the home studio was to become the center of his professional as well as his personal life.

In August 1914, while Wright was working on plans for Midway Gardens, an elaborate recreational complex in Chicago, he received tragic news. Mamah Cheney and her children, who were visiting Taliesin, along with four members of his household staff, had been murdered by a servant who had also set fire to the house. The shock and grief Wright experienced were manifested in his increasing isolation from his old life and in a premature liaison with the sculptress Miriam Noel, whose emotional instability would be a source of unhappiness for years to come. In 1915 Wright sailed with Noel for Tokyo, where he had accepted the commission to build the new Imperial Hotel. This massive

undertaking would occupy most of his time for the next seven years, during which he also maintained an office in Los Angeles.

Wright's break with the Prairie House style was manifest in the Hollyhock House, the Los Angeles residence he built for actress Aline Barnsdall between 1916 and 1920. As Manfredo Tafuri and Francesco Dal Co describe it in *Modern Architecture*: "Its massive closed forms dominate the landscape around it. Radically interlocking volumes, a heavy continuous roof, delicate decorations of Mayan inspiration aggregate in spaces disposed around a broad inner patio. Nature is brought indoors as in Oriental temples, but with reminiscences and borrowings from pre-Columbian art, thus breaking the link with the surroundings. The architecture becomes an aggregation of archaeological vestiges."

The Hollyhock House was not Wright's first commission in California. In 1909 he had successfully translated the Prairie House form into an idiom for the Pacific Coast in the George C. Stewart House in Montecito. He saw the Far West as a potential setting for the planned cities he envisioned for the future – a concept that he would continue to develop for the rest of his life. California would also be a testing ground for his interest in the pre-Columbian phase of the American experience, beginning with the Hollyhock House and continuing with the textile-block houses of the 1920s. These were constructed of precast concrete blocks that had been impressed with patterns on one or both sides,

providing a richly textured surface on both exterior and interior walls. Wright devised a system that he called "knitblock" construction, whereby parallel rows of four-inch-thick blocks, with an airspace between the two rows, were joined and reinforced by steel rods.

The first, and most successful, textile-block design was that for Alice Madison Millard, built in a wooded ravine in Pasadena in 1923. "La Miniatura," as the house was called, was a small, cubical structure overlooking a reflecting pool that replicated the richly patterned facade of concrete and the tropical foliage of the site.

Over the next two years, Wright designed larger and more imposing residences in this style for Los Angeles clients Charles Ennis, John Storer and Samuel Freeman.

The Storer House was a rectangular design with a high-ceilinged living room comparable to the two-story living room of the Millard House. Low wings carry the house out to each side. Wright supervised the construction of the house and the landscaping, which gave it the look of a Mayan temple set in a tropical forest. At this writing, it has just been completely renovated and restored.

In the Freeman House of 1924, Wright

experimented with perforated blocks inset with glass. This idea was carried forward in the house he designed for his cousin Richard Lloyd Jones in Tulsa, Oklahoma, in 1929, where glass and concrete verticals alternate. It reappeared in the 1938 design for Florida Southern College in Lakeland, in which multicolored glass was inset in concrete blocks to reflect the sunlight. This campus was Wright's only executed educational commission, apart from the Hillside Home School, designed for his aunts Jane and Nell Lloyd Wright in Spring Green in 1903. That complex would be incorporated into Taliesin during the 1930s. By that time, Wright's Wisconsin home had survived two fires – the 1914 blaze that destroyed his living quarters and a 1925 conflagration touched off by an electrical storm.

During the late 1920s, many impressive projects remained unbuilt due to the stock-market crash that announced the Depression. Among them was the innovative complex proposed for Chandler, Arizona, called San Marcos-in-the-Desert. This was to be an elegant winter resort on the order of Palm Springs, California, and Palm Beach, Florida.

By this time, Wright had divorced Catherine and married his companion, Miriam Noel, only to divorce her a year later. In 1924 he met Olgivanna Milanov, with whom he would spend the rest of his life. She was a beautiful young Montenegrin who had separated from her husband and joined the Gurdjieff Institute for the Harmonious Development of Man, in Fontainebleau. She had a young daughter, Svetlana, whom she brought to Taliesin with her early in 1925. Late that year, their daughter Iovanna was born.

As Robert C. Twombly observes in *Frank Lloyd Wright: An Interpretive Biography*, published by Harper & Row in 1973, the period between 1914 and the late 1920s was, for Wright, a time "filled with personal disaster and architectural disappointment. . . . Extensive marital and financial difficulties in the 1920s contributed to his personal and architectural doldrums long before the stock market crash affected the rest of the nation.''

In 1927 Wright and Olgivanna spent the winter in Phoenix, Arizona, while he worked on the Arizona Biltmore Hotel. The following year they were married, and Wright established the Ocotilla Camp in 1929 in Chandler, Arizona, where he was working on the project for San Marcos-in-the-Desert. This was the prototype for his future winter home in the desert, Taliesin West, built by Wright and his apprentices in the Taliesin Fellowship. Like Taliesin North, in Spring Green, the complex would be added to, enlarged, and remodeled throughout the course of Wright's life. Both these residences were to become famous and to exert a strong influence on residential design.

During his winter at Ocotilla Camp, Wright designed what he called the Chandler Block House – a small, moder-

ately priced unit to be constructed, in part, from prefabricated elements. This design would be a link between the monolithic concrete-block houses of the 1920s and the Usonian designs of the 1930s and thereafter. As Tafuri writes in *Modern Architecture*: "Now Wright was equipped to stand his ground against the International Style, to make himself the spokesman for the originality he perceived in the American cultural experience." Wright considered the International Style, as exemplified by such European architects as Ludwig Mies van der Rohe and Le Corbusier, dreary and derivative. He had a particular aversion to the International-Style skyscrapers, which he saw as filling the nation's cities with ugly glass boxes set up on stilts of concrete. His answer to the problem would evolve into the model for Broadacre City – the decentralized urban/suburban complex that he advocated tirelessly from 1935 until the end of his life. The model was con-

Right: Frank Lloyd Wright and his daughter Iovanna (by his last wife, Olgivanna Milanov), pictured in the mid-1920s.

Below: Wright poses with the model of a modern farm he designed, featured at the 1935 Industrial Arts Exhibition.

structed by student apprentices of the Taliesin Fellowship for the Industrial Arts Exhibition in New York City. In fact, this design was the only one of his planned communities to be executed, albeit on a model scale. However, the ideas behind it generated many of the Wright master-works of the 1930s, including the S. C. Johnson Company Administration Building in Racine, Wisconsin.

Just when it seemed that Wright's career was over, a host of exciting projects came to birth in the Spring Green studio. By 1932 Wright was relying on lectures and books for most of his income, since the Depression had ended so many projects for lack of money to build. The publication of the first edition of his memoirs, *An Autobiography*, in 1932, helped to revitalize interest in his ideas. (Longmans, Green & Co. published the book, which was revised and enlarged in a 1943 edition from Duell, Sloan & Pearce.) Ironically, this was the same year that Wright's work was included in an exhibition of the International Style at New York City's prestigious Museum of Modern Art.

Nineteen thirty-six brought the design of Wright's architectural masterpiece, Fallingwater, built over a stream called Bear Run in western Pennsylvania for Edgar J. Kaufmann, Sr. The soaring cantilevered balconies of this remarkable house were anchored in solid rock, and its walls were constructed of native stone laid in alternating courses. Glass, steel, and poured concrete were utilized to create a house that is completely at one with its wooded site. That same year, Wright designed the hexagonal-plan California residence called Honeycomb House for Paul and Jean Hanna near Stanford University. These buildings, and the dwelling designed for Herbert Jacobs and his wife, Katherine, in Madison, Wisconsin, represented the first Usonian houses – reflecting the social changes that had occurred in the past few decades. In his biography of Wright, Robert Twombly sums up the link between the Usonian concept and the Prairie House. Twombly writes about Wright's distinction between the plastic forms of organic architecture, which are not composed, but " 'inasmuch as they are produced by a "growing" process, they are developed and created.' From the Prairie House, wherein he tentatively achieved this unity with monomaterials and carefully placed trim, he went on in the Usonian house to merge entire rooms and floors. Continuity in his architecture manifests itself in the gradual opening up of

vistas, in the consistent treatment of materials, in horizontal lines of expression, and in the organization and flow of space, especially from the outside in."

The sensitive use of natural materials, including prefabricated components, which made the Usonian house more affordable, was another characteristic that endured throughout Wright's career. As early as 1901, in a famous lecture delivered at Hull House, in Chicago, Wright had exhorted designers to "Bring out the nature of materials, let their nature intimately into your schemes . . . reveal the nature of the wood, plaster, brick or stone in your de-

signs; they are all by nature friendly and beautiful." ("The Art and Craft of the Machine").

Wright defined the Usonian concept in *The Natural House*, published by Horizon Press in 1954. At that time, he claimed to have built more than 100 Usonian homes, but he was applying the term to all his residential designs. As originally intended, "Usonian" refers to a moderately priced house with wood, glass, and brick elements, partially prefabricated, usually of a single story, and with a slab roof. This was the kind of house he designed for the Jacobs family in 1936 and amplified in a

second dwelling to meet their changing needs in 1946.

Like the Prairie House, the Usonian was versatile. It could be designed on a square, rectangular, semicircular, or other grid to suit the site and the client's requirements. The first Jacobs House, which Wright called Usonia One, incorporated several elements of construction that would characterize the style: board-and-batten walls, a simple planning grid like that devised for the "zoned house" of earlier years, and a new form of underfloor heating through electrical coils embedded in the concrete-slab foundation.

Notable designs for Usonian houses of the late 1930s and the 1940s included those for the Ben Rebhuhn House in Great Neck, Long Island; The Pope-Leighey House in Falls Church, Virginia (subsequently moved to Mt. Vernon, Virginia); the Sidney Bazett House in Hillsborough, California; the C. Leigh Stevens House (Auldbrass Plantation) in Yemassee, South Carolina; the Gregor Affleck House in Bloomfield Hills, Michigan; and the Chauncey Griggs House in Tacoma, Washington. These houses were almost all arranged around a compact masonry core that included a fireplace and the kitchen workspace and eliminated the formal dining room. Glazed walls gave onto views of lawns and gardens behind the house, while the street facades were plain. A segmented-circle design was used for the second Jacobs House, in Middleton, Wisconsin, and reappeared in the Pearce House of 1950.

Wright had married Olgivanna Milanov in 1928, and she would remain a major influence on the architect until his death in 1959. The Taliesin Fellowship founded at Spring Green in 1932 had aspects reminiscent of such Utopian communities as New Harmony, and of the arts and crafts movement in England and Europe. The ideas

Olgivanna Wright had espoused at the Gurdjieff Institute also played a part in this community of worker-apprentices, who paid a fee to live and work with the man they considered the greatest architect of the twentieth century. Some critics applaud the planned-community principle, and the part it played in bringing Wright's projects to fruition and preserving his architectural legacy. Others are critical of the fellowship, comparing it unfavorably to the paid draftsmen who labored with Wright at the Oak Park studio, which has been compared to the Bauhaus. However, the dominant force in both of these working communities was

Frank Lloyd Wright himself, and Olgivanna Wright ensured that this situation would endure.

The last decade and a half of Wright's career brought important ecclesiastical commissions from various religious congregations, including the striking Unitarian Church in Shorewood Hills, Wisconsin; Temple Beth Sholom in Elkins Park, Pennsylvania; and the Annunciation Greek Orthodox Church in Wauwatosa, Wisconsin. In some cases Wright reworked a design that had never been built. The unexecuted project for St. Mark's Tower, in New York City (1929), eventu-

Below: The Marin County Civic Center in San Raphael, California, was designed by Wright in 1957 and completed in 1962. Distinctive features include the domed library center and the radio antenna pylon.

Opposite above: Frank Lloyd Wright, at Taliesin North. Like his design ideas, his long career was an ongoing process. When asked, what his favorite building was, Wright replied, "the next one."

Opposite below: The Kalita Humphreys Theater was designed by Wright in 1955.

Below: The Marin County Civic Center in San Raphael, California, was designed by Wright in 1957 and completed in 1962. Distinctive features include the domed library center and the radio antenna pylon.

ally became the innovative, 19-story, mixed-use Harold C. Price Company Tower in Bartlesville, Oklahoma (1953). Here the high-rise building was conceived of as a treelike structure, with a deeply sunk "taproot foundation" and cantilevered floors radiating from the central core like branches. The spiral-ramped V. C. Morris Shop in San Francisco (1948) foreshadowed the futuristic Solomon R. Guggenheim Museum in New York City – a project conceived in 1943 and plagued by innumerable delays before construction could begin in the late 1950s. Another notable design for a public building was that of the Kalita Humphreys Theater at the Dallas Theatre Center (1955).

At the same time, Wright was working on several visionary projects that were not to be executed, including the cultural complex devised for Baghdad, Iraq, in 1957. Exotic, almost playful, in its conception, the project was another unrealized fragment of Wright's great Broadacre City. His last executed building – the Marin County, California, Civic Center – was not completed until after his death, in 1962. Its long, low wings span three hills and are united by an internal road system. From the air, it could be a future city that has moved out into the landscape to provide its citizens with the air, light, space and view that Wright advocated in *The Disappearing City* of 1932 and *The Living City* of 1958. The ultimate unity – synthesis – he sought throughout his career could not be fully realized because his organic architecture was, indeed, a process and not a product.

Frank Lloyd Wright House and Studio, 1889-1909

Oak Park, Illinois

In the design of his own house and the adjacent studio, added in 1898, Wright was free to experiment with his objectives in residential architecture over a 20-year period. The original six-room shingled house, with its distinctive gables, grew with Wright's family, which eventually numbered eight people. The dining room and kitchen were enlarged considerably and equipped with the built-in shelving and storage space that Wright preferred to a motley assortment of furniture that took up space and cluttered the home environment. Other rooms were remodeled and added, including the 1893 playroom, with its barrel-vault ceiling and striking mural by Orlando Giannini above the fireplace. Continuous bands of casement windows allowed for ample light. Screens, inglenooks, and overhead lighting grids helped to define interior spaces without walling them off from each other. Furnishings and ornaments of Wright's design contribute to the atmosphere of harmony and repose that was inseparable from his sense of what a house should be.

The shingle-and-brick studio, with its entrance terrace facing Chicago Avenue, is a more fully developed exemplar of Wright's requirement for free and open spaces, multiple uses, and the connection between indoors and outdoors. Salient features include the octagonal library – a form that appeared frequently in his later work – and the two-story-high drafting room, with its balcony suspended from chains, below the clerestory windows. This drafting room was the first of Wright's many top-lighted, open-space work areas, pioneered for commercial clients in the Larkin Company and S. C. Johnson Company administration buildings.

The complex double entryway to the studio is decorated with sculptures by Richard Bock. The ubiquitous urns of this period (which one client referred to as "those flowerpots") flank the entrance. The plantings help tie the house and workplace together despite their visual disaffinity and the limitations of the site.

After Wright moved to Spring Green, Wisconsin, in 1911, he had his former property remodeled into apartments after his own design. Additional remodeling was undertaken by Clyde Nooker in 1956. Today, the Frank Lloyd Wright Home and Studio Foundation oversees the restored property – the oldest extant house by Wright – and conducts tours of the premises. The American Institute of Architects (AIA) has designated the complex one of 17 Wright buildings to be preserved as an example of his architectural contribution to American culture.

PAGES 28-29: *The west facade was part of the original house.*

OPPOSITE: *The octagonal library was added in 1898.*

ABOVE: *The dining room, with its bay window, was part of the remodeling in 1893, which also included the kitchen and second floor playroom.*

ABOVE: *The studio reception hall, with its three art glass skylights, connects the drafting room and the library.*

OPPOSITE: *The second floor playroom, with its barrel vault ceiling, was part of the 1893 remodeling.*

George Blossom House, 1892

Chicago, Illinois

A year before Wright began the independent practice of architecture, he designed the George Blossom House in the Colonial Revival style. It is a handsome example of the neoclassic New England Colonial, with its pillared portico, Palladian windows, and clapboard siding. Plane surfaces, symmetry, and geometric precision give it a sense of simple grandeur, while Wright's touch is apparent in the oblong sash windows and the low lines of the hip roof, to which dormers were added later. The arrangement of interior spaces was more open than usual in the Colonial style, reflecting Wright's determination to "beat the box," as he put it. But the house was conventional enough to spare Wright's client the jeers directed at some of his other early work, according to his recollections in *An American Architecture.*

The Blossom House was one of eight or nine commissions that Wright called his "bootlegged houses." They were designed on his own time during his five-year contract with Adler & Sullivan, but Louis Sullivan was unaware of this independent work. When he discovered it in the spring of 1893, he and Wright had a heated argument that ended their relationship for almost 20 years. Sullivan went on to break new ground in commercial architecture, culminating in the department store of Carson Pirie Scott & Company in Chicago (1899-1904). The demand for Wright's residential designs spread from suburban Chicago to other cities and states in the early 1900s, and saw the Prairie House style evolve into a major influence on international architecture.

BELOW: *On the outside, the Blossom House seems to be a typical colonial revival design.*

William H. Winslow House, 1893

River Forest, Illinois

Wright's first independent commission after leaving Adler & Sullivan was a house and stable for his friend William H. Winslow, in the Chicago suburb of River Forest. The Winslow House, on Auvergne Place, includes design elements that Wright would use throughout his long career, beginning with the foundation that ties the house to the site and suggests the stylobate that anchored a line of pillars in classical antiquity. Another characteristic feature is the predominance of the first-floor living space over the second floor, which is treated like a gallery and overhung by broad eaves. Mellow tapestry brick and white cast stone are the major building materials. The second floor has an overall foliage pattern in terra cotta in the manner of Louis Sullivan. All three of the building materials are in their natural state, unpainted and unglazed.

The entrance terrace is marked by a pair of large urns set on blocks. The original plan called for an octagonal pavilion on the south side of the house to balance the porte-cochere on the north side, but this was never built. The first floor includes a library and kitchen on the north side, living room and porch (later enclosed) on the south, and an imposing entryway and dining room in the center. Sleeping quarters are on the second floor.

The adjacent stable, with low, tiered rooflines on three levels, is a handsome structure in its own right. It was designed to provide space for Winslow's hobby – a small press for publishing noncommercial books in tasteful limited editions. In 1896, Winslow and Wright collaborated to produce a book under the Auvergne Press imprint written by a Unitarian minister named William C. Gannett. The author espoused many of the ideas about domestic life and architecture that Wright had developed as he grew up in a liberal-minded Unitarian household steeped in the transcendental tradition that dated back to Emerson and Thoreau. Wright designed and decorated the book – the forerunner of many volumes to come from his own hand on the subject of American architecture – and it was given away to friends and associates. *The House Beautiful* is now a valuable collector's item, and the Winslow House and Stable are among the 17 structures by Frank Lloyd Wright that have been designated for preservation by the American Institute of Architects.

ABOVE: *Wright's first independent commission, the Winslow House facade shows Sullivan's influence in the terra cotta decoration on the second floor.*

Robert W. Roloson Apartments,
1894

Chicago, Illinois

This was the first of several urban row-house projects designed by Wright early in his career and the only one that was executed. The client, businessman Robert W. Roloson, wanted to improve his property on Chicago's crowded South Side and increase the income from it. The four identical houses have large medieval gables and abstract stonework that makes their double row of windows a major design element. The primary building material is brown brick, but the facade of the northernmost unit has been painted over.

The interiors are designed on the mezzanine principle, so that floor heights differ between the rooms at the front and those at the back of the house. The central stairwell is the dividing point, and privacy is designed into each unit with Wright's characteristic care for this feature – a *sine qua non* of all his residential architecture.

The Roloson row-houses anticipate several features of the much later "zoned house" for the city, as proposed by Wright in the 1935 edition of *Taliesin*, an occasional publication of the Taliesin Fellowship. In that issue, he wrote: "the town house is tall; all rooms have high ceilings. The entire house is hermetically sealed from dirt and noise. . . . The slumber zone is introduced as mezzanine with balcony opening into the living kitchen" (a feature associated with the Usonian house concept dating from the 1930s). In the plan outlined in *Taliesin*, the city house has no windows at all and is air-conditioned throughout. A utility stack houses all the wiring, plumbing and heating components, and outdoor living space is built into the rooftop, "where greenery can see the sky," as Wright put it. His predilection for roof gardens would endure into the 1950s, when he proposed to include one in the design for the Solomon R. Guggenheim Museum in New York City, but was voted down by the curator.

The entrances of the Roloson Apartments, like those of many Wright buildings of this period, are innocuous and unspectacular.

Nathan G. Moore House, 1895
Oak Park, Illinois

About a year after he completed the innovative – and often maligned – Winslow House, Wright was approached for a design by attorney Nathan G. Moore, who lived across the street from Wright's home and studio. Moore was eager to build a house in the newly popular half-timbered Tudor style, and Wright was willing to nod to convention because he needed the job. In fact, the Moore House was a bold variation on the Tudor style, with steeply angled peaked roofs, richly ornamented exterior woodwork, and narrow dormer windows tucked into odd corners along the roofline.

To Wright's chagrin, the Moore House was widely admired, and he was besieged by requests for Tudor mansions like Moore's. He had designed the house to some extent with tongue in cheek, especially when he added a distinctly American front porch to the dwelling that managed somehow not to seem obtrusive. But the house was so well received that Wright claimed he could have made a career of designing half-timbered buildings against his inclinations.

As we see it today, the house incorporates new design elements, primarily Japanese, that were added by Wright after it was gutted by fire in 1922 and the Moores asked him to rebuild it above the first floor. Wright's design reflected his interest in what he called "The lands of my dreams – old Japan and old Germany."

The Moore House is located just north of Wright's Edward R. Hills House (1906) – commissioned by Nathan Moore for his daughter and son-in-law – and across the street from the Arthur Heurtley House (1902).

ABOVE: *A traditional gothic window in the Moore House stands in contrast to the Japanese-influenced windows on the second floor, designed by Wright in 1922.*

OPPOSITE: *The facade features many typical early Wright details, including ornamental urns and stonework.*

PAGES 40-41: *A steeply pitched roof and wide chimney identify the Nathan G. Moore House.*

ABOVE: *Decorative brickwork and stonework on the facade of the Francisco Terrace Apartments was still evident shortly before its demolition in 1974.*

OPPOSITE: *The entrance arch has been built into a new apartment complex which imitates Wright's original facade, but eliminates the corner staircase towers and interior porches.*

Francisco Terrace Apartments,
1895 (demolished 1974)
Chicago, Illinois

Francisco Terrace was one of two apartment projects designed and built for Edward C. Waller in 1895. Waller was a neighbor of Wright's friend and client William H. Winslow, for whom he built the River Forest residence that anticipated the Prairie House. Waller, in turn, became an important client and patron.

The two-story brick complex that Wright designed for the corner of Francisco and West Walnut streets was innovative in that all the apartments except those facing the street opened onto a rectangular courtyard reached through a terracotta archway. The spandrels of the archway are decorated with a foliage pattern reminiscent of Sullivan. A wooden balcony gave the apartments access to the court through stairways in open towers at each corner of the building. The ground-floor apartments had wooden porches on the courtyard. The main disadvantage of the plan was the incessant noise caused by traffic on the balcony and amplified by the court. Like many of the buildings that Wright would design for urban use, including the Larkin Company Administration Building in Buffalo, New York, Francisco Terrace seemed to turn its back on the surrounding neighborhood, giving it a closed, fortresslike feeling. It was designed as a kind of model tenement, within the reach of working-class renters, but the ideal was not fully realized.

Around the corner, on Jackson Boulevard and Kedzie Avenue, were the more expensive Waller Apartments, whose construction was not supervised by Wright. These five, two-story brick units were identical in floor plan, but their entrance details varied. Both Francisco Terrace and the Waller Apartments fell into a state of disrepair due to neglect, and the Terrace was demolished in 1974. By that time, the building had been defaced by vandalism, and an ugly board-and-wire fence ran along the street side. Unfortunately, the complex had come to resemble "the sanitary slum" that Wright often deplored. The imposing entrance arch was dismantled and reconstructed on Euclid Place, in Oak Park, in 1977.

Isidore Heller House, 1896

Chicago, Illinois

The I-shaped, three-story Heller House was designed for a narrow city lot on Chicago's South Woodlawn Avenue. It has walls of Roman brick and the tile roofs in the monitor style, whereby a small third story surmounts the main roof, which covers the first two stories. The third-story loggia, pierced by open arcades, has a plaster frieze, each panel of which bears a human figure in high relief. The sculptor was Richard Bock, with whom Wright would collaborate on many projects.

On the ground floor, the reception room opens into a long hall that runs east to west. It connects the large rectangular spaces of the living and dining room on a cruciform plan that would reappear in many of the Prairie Houses. Low chimneys rise from either end of the roof. The original plans called for a stable immediately adjacent to the house, but apparently, it was never built.

The loggia seems out of place because it makes the house so tall in proportion to its width. In this instance, Wright violated his own dictum about horizontality to the detriment of the design. The lack of view from this site makes a third story problematic and runs counter to Wright's advice, in the book *Modern Architecture*, that "the house should have repose and

such texture as will quiet the whole and make it graciously at one with external nature." The external nature available on the average city lot could not be compared to the ambient lawns and trees that graced the suburban lots where Wright built most of his designs at this period.

ABOVE: *The facade and doorway of the Heller House are decorated with stone columns typical of the period, a style Wright would soon abandon.*

Joseph Husser House, 1899
(demolished 1926)
Chicago, Illinois

The Husser House came from Wright's drawing board at a time when he was embarking upon a full decade of intense creativity. The Prairie-House style is foreseen here in a wealth of features. First, the basement of the residence was at ground level, rather than excavated, and the house rose another two stories to overlook a panoramic view of nearby Lake Michigan. The cruciform plan was fully realized in the extensions to east and west, respectively, the dining room overlooking the lake and the entry stairwell.

On the second (main) floor, the rectangular portion of the house comprised a large octagonal porch, a spacious living room, and the study, kitchen, and servants' rooms. The third floor, with its ornamentation in the style of Sullivan, contained the

sleeping quarters.

The principal construction material was plaster, with bands of wood trim. The broad eaves overhanging the house gave the imposing structure a sense of shelter and prevented the long north-south extension from appearing monumental.

Unfortunately, as Chicago overflowed its former boundaries, new buildings between the house and Lake Michigan spoiled the view from the Husser House and hemmed it in on all sides. Although the structure was demolished, the furniture and fittings designed by Wright were preserved. The dining room he produced for the Husser House, with table and eight chairs, was auctioned in 1987 for $1.6 million – a record price for twentieth-century decorative art.

RIGHT: *A close-up view of the central core of the Husser House, demolished in 1926, shows the ornamental sculpture on the third floor.*

Frank Wright Thomas House
(The Harem), 1901
Oak Park, Illinois

This two-story residence was the first Prairie-style house in Oak Park, where Wright designed some 40 houses, many of them for friends and acquaintances. There is no excavated basement under the L-shaped dwelling, and the ground floor contains all the family living areas.

The bedrooms are on the second floor, where the casement windows are more widely spaced than those on the main floor. The extended rooflines of the lower story project over the porch and dining room at either end of the L. The chimney, low and massive, is designed to ventilate the air spaces beneath the roofs in hot weather by means of openings that could be closed for the winter.

Entrance from the sidewalk is through an exotic archway flanked by low stone walls. The site plan included a large rec-

tangular garden at the rear of the house. Original construction was of plaster on wood frame, but for many years the exterior was shingled. In 1975 the original plaster surface of the house was restored.

The Thomas House was commissioned by James C. Rogers, who made a gift of it to his daughter and son-in-law, Mr. and Mrs. Frank W. Thomas. Oak Park neighbors nicknamed the house "The Harem," because of its vaguely Moorish-looking entrance arch and its raised living quarters. In fact, the house was incongruent with the conventional Queen Anne-style residence next door, but Wright was accustomed to working with small suburban lots and he often made no account of what went on beyond his client's property line. Neighbors with more conventional houses had to shift for themselves.

LEFT: *The restored plaster façade accentuates the horizontal details of the early Prairie House.*

BELOW: *The living room includes a large brick fireplace without a mantel, built-in cupboards and a plate rail.*

Ward W. Willits House, 1901

Highland Park, Illinois

The Willits House consolidated the primary design elements that Wright had been exploring in his work since 1893. Its elegant simplicity gave it the "new sense of repose in flat planes and quiet streamline effects" that Wright identified in his autobiography as the goals of organic architecture. Some critics consider the Willits

House the first – and one of the finest – in the mature Prairie style.

Wood and steel were the primary construction materials, with exterior plastering and wood trim. The foundation and base course are cement. All the living quarters are raised above ground level. The end wall of the living room is glazed, look-

ing into a large terrace and the grounds, thus uniting house to site in a new way that would characterize Wright's designs for the future.

The wings of the house fan out like a pinwheel from the central core – a massive fireplace with wood screening that identified the various functions of the ground-

floor spaces without limiting them. Entry hall, living room, dining room, and kitchen adjoined by servants' rooms, make up the main floor. The porte-cochere extending from the entry-hall wing is balanced by the long porch off the dining room.

Casement windows placed high in the walls admit light from above and focus the eye on the sky rather than the immediate environs of the house. The underside of the roof projections is flat and light in color, to reflect light into the bedrooms on the second floor. The large, low chimney identifies the central fireplace as the heart of the house – an abiding characteristic in Wright's residential designs throughout his career.

The Willits House is a giant step forward into Wright's ideal of open space under shelter without the constraints imposed by traditional boxlike construction. As such, it is one of the 17 Wright buildings designated for preservation by the AIA.

William G. Fricke House, 1901

Oak Park, Illinois

The three-story Fricke House bears the stamp of Wright's early determination to be master of both concept and design in the projects he undertook. Although he acknowledged the importance of the machine to modern life, and incorporated complex new systems of heating, lighting and ventilation into his buildings, as in the Fricke House, they are anything but mechanistic. His overriding concern with disassembling and reassembling the traditional box-for-living is clearly articulated in this design, which resembles that of the William E. Martin House of the previous year. Both could be called Cubist in the handling of the clean-cut geometric forms – rectangular, octagonal and square – that are fitted together to form the building. Some of these shapes are open-ended, others are closed.

The three tiers of the roofline are balanced by the two large chimneys that mark the top story. Balance, in fact, is the keynote of the building, and the tension created in working toward it is implicit in almost every Wright design.

In *Many Masks*, Brendan Gill discusses Wright's unacknowledged debt to German and Austrian architects like Joseph Maria Olbrich, whose work was well known to Wright and his colleagues. In fact, when Wright traveled to Europe in 1909 to work on the Wasmuth portfolio, he was introduced as "the American Olbrich." Both of these gifted young men were working toward the same goal – a contemporary style independent of the past and its manifold accretions. In Wright's case, there was also a strong drive toward independence of others in his field. He frequently denigrated their work and minimized their accomplishments, even when he had a grudging admiration for them.

The three-story Fricke House is one of the tallest Wright designs in Oak Park, Illinois.

Arthur Heurtley House, 1902

Oak Park, Illinois

This house, only a block from Wright's home and studio in Oak Park, was commissioned at the same time as a remodeling of the Heurtley summer cottage on Marquette Island, Michigan. The plan of the house is square, and the living quarters are all above ground. Living rooms, kitchen, and family bedrooms were placed on the main floor, with guest rooms and bath, playroom, and servants' quarters on the ground floor. (The house has since been remodeled into two apartments.)

A new note is struck by the brick exterior, laid in horizontal courses that suggest board and batten. The arched entryway is sheltered by a low pierced wall surmounted by urns. (Wright frequently designed apertures into his walls and eaves to admit patterned light that enhanced the texture and shading of the surface.) What he called a "light screen" of continuous casement windows set high in the walls provides an unbroken outdoor vista from the main floor.

The influence of the Japanese print on Wright's designs may be discerned in the clean, uncluttered lines of the house, securely anchored to the site by its concrete foundation line. The dappled shade cast by overhanging branches brings out the solid linear quality of the masonry, with its warm earth tones. The walls are of tawny Roman brick, their courses projecting at regular intervals to form a pattern. This is an example of Wright's concern that decorative features be integral to the design, rather than imposed upon it later like icing from a pastry tube. The same philosophy holds true for the interior of the house, with its many Wright-designed features. Years after he built the widely admired Heurtley House, Wright wrote an article for the London *Architect's Journal* in which he acknowledged the influence of Japanese art, stating that the prints he had studied and collected were "a lesson in elimination of the insignificant and in the beauty of the natural use of materials."

LEFT: *The projecting courses of brick in the facade emphasize the horizontal qualities of the building.*

BELOW LEFT: *An early photograph of the living room shows an angular display cabinet and the broad fireplace.*

Susan Lawrence Dana House,
1902
Springfield, Illinois

Susan Lawrence Dana was an art collector and a socialite descended from one of Springfield's earliest families. In 1902 she commissioned Wright to create a large new house around an existing house that was too small to display her collection or to entertain in on a lavish scale.

The original house was incorporated – some say engulfed in – the imposing brick structure that Wright designed, along with all its furniture and fittings. The project took two years to complete, and in 1905 Wright was invited to add the Lawrence Memorial Library, connected to the house by a raised walkway.

The naturalistic motif used effectively throughout the house was an abstract pattern derived from the prairie sumac; it appears in the detailing of items as diverse as window glass, lighting fixtures, rugs and murals.

This was the first of Wright's houses to contain two-story rooms: the gallery, dining room, and hall. The gallery served as a showcase and reception room for members of the artistic community. It is connected to the house by a covered passage that doubled as a conservatory. Sculptor Richard Bock, artist George Niedecken, and the Linden Glass Company all collaborated with Wright on the project.

The Dana House has a cruciform plan, with all the principal common rooms on the main floor and the bedrooms and offices upstairs. Numerous balconies and loggias overlook the raised terrace on the street side of the house, the grounds, and the extensive garden off the gallery.

The interior walls are of cream-colored brick, and the woodwork is red oak. The lofty plaster ceilings were sand-finished and ribbed with wood. Wherever possible, furniture and fixtures were built in to maximize floor space and contribute to a restful, uncluttered look. The austere facade, with its arched entryway approached by broad, shallow steps to the terrace, was softened by foliage cascading from the balconies and urns on the terrace walls.

To some critics, the Dana House has appeared grandiose and overwrought. Undeniably, it looks much more like a public building than a residence, even apart from the library building that was added in 1905. It was the most elaborate Prairie-style house of its time, and Wright and his collaborators had a free hand – and a generous budget – with which to create the integrated environment he envisioned.

BELOW: *The rooflines of the Dana House are emphasized by copper eaves colored by the characteristic green patina – a quality which Wright admired.*

OPPOSITE: *The second floor of the Dana House is decorated with a geometric frieze.*

RIGHT: *The designs of many of the windows in the Dana House are based on such native plants as the prairie sumac.*

BELOW: *One of the five fireplaces in the house is decorated with tile and a pattern of butterflies carved in the granite surround.*

OPPOSITE: *The two-story dining room with a barrel vault features a delicate frieze by George Neidecken.*

The fountain in the reception area, The
Moon Children *by Richard Bock, is
surrounded by art glass windows and doors
leading to a rear hallway.*

Stained art glass panels in window frames acted as screens, allowing light to enter the house, but still maintaining a sense of privacy.

William E. Martin House, 1902

Oak Park, Illinois

Wright carried out half a dozen commissions for the Martin brothers, William and Darwin, in the early 1900s, including the E-Z Polish Factory building in Chicago. The three-story Prairie-style house that Wright designed for William Martin in Oak Park bears some resemblance to the nearby Fricke House, especially in its large size and in the plaster-and-wood trim. However, its plan is more clearly articulated, and interior space flows more freely. Good use was made of the large, level building lot, and the grounds were beautifully landscaped. In fact, the house is more successful in both conception and execution than the larger, more expensive house that Wright designed for William's brother Darwin in Buffalo, New York. It has been suggested that this is mainly because William Martin took Wright's design as he found it, while his brother insisted on numerous changes that compromised the quality of the project.

The main-floor plan for the Oak Park house included an entrance hall, library, living and dining rooms, and a kitchen adjoined by servants' quarters. (Wright's disdain for both attics and cellars was a blessing to people who worked for his clients as domestics. It got them out of the

sweltering eaves and damp basements that usually contained the servants' quarters in traditional houses.) There were two large porches, one of which projected into the sizable garden, with its paths, pond, bridge, and a pergola leading to a tennis court. The second porch faced the street. The third floor contained bedrooms and baths opening off a cruciform central hall.

As in the Willits House, all the living quarters are above ground level, and broad, light-colored eaves projecting over bands of casement windows help to illuminate the upper stories. The single large chimney is typical of the Prairie House.

For some years, the house was subdivided into three apartments, but in 1945 it was sensitively restored to serve as a single-family dwelling.

ABOVE: *The three-story William E. Martin House built of plaster and wood is similar to the Fricke House and typical of the Prairie style.*

OPPOSITE TOP: *The living room features a built-in inglenook seat near the fireplace.*

OPPOSITE BOTTOM: *The open plan of the first floor seems to increase the space allotted to each downstairs room.*

Edwin H. Cheney House, 1903

Oak Park, Illinois

The house Wright designed for Edwin and Mamah Borthwick Cheney is a single-story brick residence with wood trim and an excavated basement. One enters from the street side by way of a brick-walled terrace that turns left before it reaches the front entrance and is all but invisible from view. This indirect approach to a building was a frequent factor in Wright's designs, including that of his Oak Park studio. It has the effect of heightening the sense of house as shelter vis-à-vis the outside world while creating the expectation of something rare and unusual within.

The entrance hall opens on one side to a long living room and on the other to a corridor that separates the sleeping quarters from the living areas. The house has more space than its appearance suggests: a study, five bedrooms, several dressing rooms, and a long verandah. The basement rooms were designed for use as utility rooms, including storage and laundry. Originally, the Cheney House was surrounded by gardens that included a fountain with built-in stone benches.

It was in the course of designing and building this house that Wright and Mrs. Cheney formed the attachment that would eventually lead to their elopement to Europe in 1909. The scandal that ensued effectively ended the first phase of Wright's career along with his marriage to Catherine Wright.

BELOW: *The Cheney House seems protected by its terrace, which accentuates the private quality of the house.*

BOTTOM: *The high ceiling of the Cheney House adds light and space to the interior living room.*

Hillside Home School (Nell and Jane Lloyd Jones), 1903

Spring Green, Wisconsin

The original Hillside Home School – essentially a roomy house – was designed by Wright in 1887 for his aunts, Nell and Jane Lloyd Jones, in rural Spring Green, Wisconsin. As Wright was apprenticed at that time to Joseph Lyman Silsbee, who had a hand in the design, the shingled, gable-roofed structure owed much to Silsbee's influence. The house remained in use until 1950, when it was demolished. The complex that Wright built for the Lloyd Jones sisters in 1903 is entirely of his design, constructed of native sandstone and solid oak timber. Inside the H-shaped building, the walls are sandstone below and plastered above, framed in exposed oak timbers.

The spacious, open floor plan provided for six classrooms, a gymnasium, an assembly hall, and a skylighted laboratory and art studio. The two sides of the building were connected by a long gallery. The library was housed in a large balcony.

Continuous oblong windows on the surrounding countryside, and plantings raised on outside screens and piers, obviated the drab institutional look of traditional school buildings, in keeping with the family's progressive ideas on education. The plan provided for what Wright described as "enclosing screens and protecting features of architectural character that took the place of the solid wall" (*Two Lectures on Architecture*, The Art Institute of Chicago, 1931).

When the Taliesin Fellowship was

formed in 1932, the Hillside Home School, then in an advanced state of disrepair, was extensively remodeled into a complex to provide working quarters and housing for the apprentices, in conjunction with Wright's property at Taliesin. It was here that Wright and members of the fellowship began work on his concept for future urban planning in the model for Broadacre City. Only this scale model was fully realized, although various residential and commercial projects of the 1930s and early 1940s were incorporated to illustrate the principles that Wright hoped to see widely applied.

TOP: *Wright's design for Hillside Home School (seen from the south) set the building, constructed of native rock and plaster, at the top of a gentle slope.*

ABOVE: *The gallery connecting the two main buildings was reduced to a single story when the school was remodeled in 1932.*

*The sculpture on the exterior piers of the
Larkin Building was designed by Richard
Bock.*

64 LARKIN COMPANY ADMINISTRATION BUILDING

Larkin Company Administration Building, 1903

(demolished 1949-50)
Buffalo, New York

Wright's commissions in Buffalo, including the Larkin Building, resulted from his acquaintance with businessman William E. Martin, a neighbor and client in Oak Park. The Larkin Company was a successful mail-order business founded by John Larkin and his brother-in-law Elbert Hubbard. When Hubbard retired from the enterprise, William Martin's brother, Darwin D. Martin, took his place.

Apart from his own studio in Oak Park, the Larkin Building was Wright's first example of a large, open workplace in the style of an atrium, lighted from above. Fulfillment of all the company's orders was carried out in this central atrium; supervisors and executives occupied separate offices in tiered galleries on either side. Utilities and stairways were housed in large shafts outside the corners of the building to conserve interior space. Wright designed all the metal furniture and fittings, including file cabinets, which were emplaced under the seven-foot-high windows on each floor.

Wright's customary concern with ventilation and good lighting resulted in the first commercial use of air conditioning and plate glass in this structure. As the building was located in Buffalo's noisy, sooty factory district, Wright sought to create a clean, quiet environment independent of its surroundings. Fresh air was taken in from shafts on the roof and circulated through pipes in the four utility wells. The building materials were fireproof, primarily brick, with cream-colored brick and magnesite on the interior.

The exterior was massive and severe, its only ornament being sculptured piers at either end of the main blocks that corresponded to the boundaries of the atrium inside. Entrance was from annexes facing the streets at each end and connected to the main lobby. Many critics objected to the Larkin Building's monolithic look, and it is likely that the company's employees took some time to get used to it. However, Wright contended that the building's form was integrated to its function. He was quick to say that it had "the same claim to consideration as a 'work of art' as an ocean liner, or a locomotive, or a battleship."

The Larkin Building finally outlived its usefulness and was demolished in 1949-50. Wright took some satisfaction in the amount of time and money that was required to bring the "battleship" down. Remnants of a single pier are still visible on the site.

Wright also designed the desks, chairs and light fixtures for the Larkin Building.

Unity Temple, 1904
Oak Park, Illinois

The Wrights were members of the Unitarian congregation in Oak Park, and when its Gothic Revival church burned down in 1904, the building committee asked Wright to design its replacement. However, even the historically open-minded and progressive Unitarians were perplexed by the concrete monolith that began to take form on the corner of Lake Street and Kenilworth Avenue. It was like no church they had ever seen before. The walls were of poured concrete and rose steeply over the suburban setting, flanked by massive piers at each corner, reminiscent of those in the Larkin Building, that housed stairways and storage space.

In his text for the Wasmuth portfolio of his early works (1910), Wright described the building as "A concrete monolith cast in wooden forms. After removal of forms,

exterior surfaces washed clean to expose the small gravel aggregate, the finished result not unlike a coarse granite." The columns and architectural ornaments were of the same material. There was a common entrance to the church and the social hall, Unity House, which Wright called "the good-time place." Both parts of the building were lighted from above by bands of windows marking off the interior space from the coffered glass ceiling. Wright also designed the globed chandeliers and the other fixed furnishings. The roofs were waterproof reinforced-concrete slabs.

The great achievement of Unity Temple is the interior of the church. Here, weight-bearing volumes are cleanly defined in space etched out by the slender wooden uprights. A sense of intimacy between speaker and audience is achieved by pro-

jecting the podium into the congregation. The effect of top lighting, both natural and artificial, is at once remarkably bright and restful.

The exterior of the building has been resurfaced, so it is no longer possible to see the successive layers of concrete as they were poured into the forms from day to day. However, Unity Temple remains an imposing presence as an entirely new kind of space for communal use. It bears the epigraph: "For the worship of God and the service of man."

ABOVE LEFT: *The cement facade of Unity Temple insulated the congregation from the disturbance and noise of the nearby trolley line.*

FAR LEFT: *The room is lit naturally by second story windows and coffered skylights set with amber glass.*

LEFT: *The double balconies in alcoves around the room bring the congregation closer to the pulpit and the minister.*

Darwin D. Martin House, 1904
Buffalo, New York

The house that Wright designed for Darwin D. Martin while the Larkin Building was under construction was to be his most ambitious residential project to that date. Martin thought highly of Wright's abilities, but the two wrangled constantly about cost overruns, lagging schedules, and Wright's insistence on controlling every aspect of the project.

The prototype for the Martin House was Wright's design for "A Home in a Prairie Town," provided to editor Edward Bok for publication in the *Ladies' Home Journal* in 1901. However, the generous Martin budget made it possible to build the house on a much grander scale than that portrayed in the popular women's magazine. Plans for the Martin House included a pergola, conservatory, stable, garage and a smaller house on one corner of the property. This was rented by Martin's sister and brother-in-law, Mr. and Mrs. George Barton. It has been suggested that the small but elegant Barton House is superior to the mansion designed for the Martins.

The ground floor of the main house included a very large living room opening onto the dining room and a huge covered porch. A reception room doubled as a small living room, and there was an office, a library and a kitchen. The pergola was enclosed by glass and afforded a hundred-foot perspective from the main hall. Upstairs were the family and guest bedrooms. The grounds were tastefully landscaped with expensive plantings and the oversized urns that were to crop up in Wright's designs throughout his career.

The small Barton House was much lighter inside than the main house, where the large covered porch shut off the sun to the living room. Its manageable size made it much more homelike than the Martin House, which ended up costing nearly $100,000 – a huge sum for the time. Essentially a Prairie House in style, the Martin House became rather too large and complex for what Wright called the grammar of this kind of structure.

The Darwin D. Martin House, a Prairie-style design built on the T-plan, has a porte-cochere and sheltered front entrance.

Thomas P. Hardy House, 1905
Racine, Wisconsin

Wright's talents found new scope in a design for the precipitous site of the Hardy House, built on a bluff overlooking Lake Michigan. Up until this time, most of his residential commissions had been for houses on level suburban lots, many of them flanked by traditional houses that jarred with his innovative designs. However, the Hardy House was to occupy its vertical site alone, except for the conventional houses that faced it (disapprovingly) across South Main Street. In fact, the house was generally derided in Racine – even by future Wright clients like Herbert "Hib" Johnson of the Johnson Wax Company, who passed it every day on his way to work.

Small, simple and elegant, the Hardy House rises from its site like a graceful ornament: "not *on* the hill but *of* the hill," as Wright often said of his site plans, including those for Taliesin North. The house is almost Japanese in its use of tall, white unadorned panels marked off by dark timbering.

The roof has simple pediments centering on low ridges. Wright generally disavowed his debt to Japanese architecture, which he had seen at first hand in the Japanese pavilion at the World's Columbian Exposition. However, he had always been interested in Orientalia and was an early and avid collector of Japanese prints.

"During my later years at the Oak Park workshop," he wrote in his autobiography, "Japanese prints had intrigued me and taught me much. . . . A process of simplification in art in which I was myself already engaged, beginning with my twenty-third year, found much collateral evidence in the print."

Eventually, Wright would purchase Japanese prints not only for his own collection but for major museums, including New York's Metropolitan Museum of Art, the Museum of Fine Arts in Boston, and the Art Institute of Chicago. The tall, vertical perspective for the Hardy House, drawn freehand in ink, is an excellent example of what Wright had learned from the artists of the Japanese woodblock.

OPPOSITE: *The terrace that faces the lakeside is below the level of the street.*

ABOVE: *The height of the two-story living room is accentuated by the simple outlined wall panels.*

Frederick C. Robie House, 1906

Chicago, Illinois

The best-known of all Wright's houses in the Prairie style was built on a narrow corner lot in Chicago. The house was commissioned in 1906 by Frederick C. Robie, a successful young inventor who manufactured automobile supplies. Robie won Wright's interest immediately when he approached the architect for a contemporary house design that would take advantage of new technology. He was eager to have Wright design all the furnishings, plantings, and utility systems required and was willing to spend whatever was necessary.

The Robie House extends along a single horizontal axis, its most arresting feature being the cantilevered roof, which extends a full 20 feet beyond the masonry supports. The long, low structure is built entirely of brick and concrete, free of ornamentation. The front door cannot even be seen from the street. The various porches and balconies that provide access to the outside on several levels have been compared to the prows and decks of a ship. There was no porte-cochere like those that Wright included in most of his designs at this time. Instead, the garage was integral to the building.

Inside, the Robie House was revolutionary in having no walls or partitions to break the flow of space through the common areas: living room, dining room, and central stairwell. The chimney serves as a screen, not a divider, and the space continues into diamond-shaped bays at either end of the house, opening onto porches. Bedrooms, kitchen and servants' quarters were placed at the rear of the house. The ground-floor level contained a children's playroom, a billiard, or recreation, room, and the boiler room and laundry. The walled courtyard was an extension of the children's playroom.

The inventive Robie contributed many ideas, which resulted in extremely efficient lighting, telephone and alarm systems, as well as an industrial vacuum-cleaning system. Wright designed all the furniture, fabrics and fittings, including the globular lighting fixtures and the art glass for windows and French doors. In fact, the finished house did resemble an imposing steamship, or *Dampfer*, which is what Chicago's German-speaking people called it. The Robie House cost the then-prohibitive sum of $60,000. Many students of modern architecture consider it the highest achievement of what has been called Wright's First Golden Age.

ABOVE: *The square concrete courses edging the terrace accentuate the horizontal design of the Robie House.*

OPPOSITE: *Many typical Wright designs, including decorative glass and deep overhanging eaves, were incorporated in the Robie House.*

PAGES 74-75: *The living room of the Robie House features a fireplace with a lowered hearth and off-center flue.*

Avery Coonley House, 1907
Riverside, Illinois

It was Wright's good fortune to have an-other ideal client like Fred Robie in the person of Avery Coonley, who gave his architect a free hand and a liberal budget. The elegant variation on the Prairie House theme that Wright executed for the Coon-leys along the Des Plaines River is one of his grandest essays in residential design. The main house (the Playhouse was added in 1912) has no excavated basement; its ground floor serves that function, provi-ding space for utilities and a large play-room opening onto a terrace with an orna-mental pool. As in the Robie House, the unobtrusive main entrance gives onto a dark hall at this level, where a flight of stairs leads to the second (main) floor, which is, by contrast, even lighter and more open.

All the main rooms of the house are on the second level, overlooking lawns and garden from various heights in a system of joined pavilions. Large, harmonious vistas mark the flow of space from one living area to another, and the ceilings were brought down to a human scale, enhancing the sense of shelter. In the *Architect's Journal* of London (Summer 1936), Wright recalled the satisfaction he had felt in the design of

the Coonley House: "Freedom of floor space and the elimination of useless heights worked a miracle in the new dwell-ing place. A sense of appropriate freedom had changed its whole aspect. The dwell-ing became more fit for human habitation and more natural to its site."

The exterior of the house has a banded effect – plaster below and ceramic inlaid in stucco above. The effect is both exotic and serene. The entire complex benefits from its idyllic surroundings in the community of Riverside, which was laid out by Fred-erick Law Olmstead, the creator of New York City's Central Park, in 1869. Resi-dents of this wealthy suburb were willing to pay for the best of both worlds: an en-vironment of unspoiled natural beauty in close proximity to downtown Chicago by efficient means of transportation.

ABOVE: *The exterior of the Coonley House is decorated with a frieze of colored tile.*

OPPOSITE TOP: *The Coonley Playhouse, constructed in 1912, contained a small stage, assembly and work rooms.*

OPPOSITE BOTTOM: *An early photograph of the interior of the Coonley Playhouse shows the window and furniture designed by Wright.*

F. F. Tomek House, 1907

Riverside, Illinois

The Tomek House, built in the expensive suburb of Riverside, Illinois, is a long, low Prairie-style structure that served as a prototype for the Robie House, built in 1908-09. The ground floor is essentially a raised basement, primarily for storage, heating and laundry facilities. The second level houses the main family living areas, and the bedrooms are above. The house has no attic, which was the norm in Wright's designs.

The eaves of the house are very broadly cantilevered and add impressiveness to the entrance, with its heavy piers on either side. The many windows of the second level give ample light to the principal rooms and allow an unimpeded view of trees and sky. Unfortunately, most of the ground-level space, usually designated "billiard room" or "children's playroom"

in designs of this period, was effectively wasted because of low light and general inconvenience of access. As the years went by, these raised basements became increasingly expensive to build and impossible to justify in view of the shrinking size of the American family and the virtual disappearance of domestic help.

With all its amenities of site and space, the Tomek House and others like it were soon to become anachronistic, even for the affluent, upper-middle-class families for which they were designed. They would be superseded in Wright's work of the 1930s and thereafter by the smaller, less expensive, partly prefabricated Usonian houses that reworked the Prairie House elements into a new kind of dwelling that reflected the social and economic changes going on in the nation at large.

LEFT: *The deep eaves and horizontal trim are Wright designs that mark the similarities of this house and the Robie House.*

BELOW: *The living room, with its central fireplace, is connected to the rest of the house by a narrow but well-lit corridor.*

Meyer May House, 1908
Grand Rapids, Michigan

The Meyer May House, on a spacious suburban lot in Grand Rapids, is an excellent example of the results obtained when Wright was entrusted with total design responsibility for a project. Here he was able to implement the ideas about unity that he would describe the following year in his text for the Wasmuth portfolio, *Ausgeführte Bauten und Entwürfe von Frank Lloyd Wright*:

"It is quite impossible to consider the building one thing, and its furnishings another, its setting and environs still another. In the spirit in which these buildings are conceived, these are all one thing, to be foreseen and provided for in the nature of the structure. . . . Heating apparatus, light-ing fixtures, the very chairs and tables, cabinets and musical instruments, where practicable, are of the building itself."

A walk through the warm and inviting May House discloses a harmonious blend of burnished woodwork; softly diffused light from symmetrical fixtures, chandeliers, and recessed panels; art-glass windows whose motif is echoed in carpets and textiles throughout the house. In the hall is a glowing hollyhock mural by artist George Neidecken in various shades of gold. The dining room table has a pier at each corner surmounted by a lamp. The chairs are of the severe-looking, high-backed design Wright favored – although even he finally admitted that they were uncomfortable (a defect shared by some of the office furniture he would design for future commercial projects). The living room is serene and uncluttered, with built-in bookcases and padded benches. The focal point is the oversize fireplace with its three tiers of brickwork. Armchairs and cabinets are clean-lined and functional.

As the first phase of Wright's career drew to a close, and his ideas began to exert more and more influence on other architects, the synthesis he achieved in works like the May, Robie and Coonley houses showed the worth of the principles of organic architecture that he had espoused for 20 years.

ABOVE: *The exterior of the house shows Wright's use of ornamental lattice which screens the first floor windows from the street.*

OPPOSITE: *The design of the glass shades on the corner posts of the table duplicates the windows which fill two sides of the room.*

PAGES 82-83: *Deep eaves cover the extensive terraces surrounding the Meyer May House.*

Mrs. Thomas H. Gale House, 1909

Oak Park, Illinois

The Gale House is another of those designed by Wright for friends and neighbors in Oak Park, where it is still a great distinction to own a house by Frank Lloyd Wright. This is a compact, harmonious design that has been compared to that of the Edgar J. Kaufmann Sr., House, Fallingwater. The Gale House balcony jutting out over the ground-floor porch, and the tiered roofline, do suggest the cantilevered terraces of the tri-level house on Bear Run that most critics consider Wright's masterpiece. But the Gale House is primarily a Prairie House rather than a Usonian, and is similar to the several projects that Wright had designed for the *Ladies' Home Journal* in 1901.

The familiar stylobate at ground level, the bands of windows above and below, the low roofline in harmony with surrounding trees and the sky, open porches and garden walls that extend the house more fully into the site – all these are typical of Wright's residential designs of the early 1900s. Less tangible, but no less important, is the aura of privacy and self-containment that Wright built into these houses, with their various spaces fitted into one another in a variety of ways tailored to the needs of each client. Wright's ideas on family life were, in fact, idealistic, and closely tied to his Utopian view of how citizens of a democracy should live: untrammeled by peremptory boundaries and sharing both space and activities while allowing for full development of the individual. Each of his houses is unique in the way it seeks to express this ideal. As Wright put it in 1912, in his book *The Japanese Print: An Interpretation*: "Art is not alone the expression, but in turn the great conservator and transmitter of the finer sensibilities of a people."

ABOVE: *The house Wright built for Mrs. Thomas H. Gale is marked by an early use of cantilever design.*

Taliesin North, 1911-1959

Spring Green, Wisconsin

After Wright's break with suburban Oak Park, he undertook to build the country house and studio he called Taliesin, from the Welsh for "shining brow." His mother had purchased the hillside property among her relatives in southwestern Wisconsin during Wright's extended stay in Europe (1909-11). It was in sight of the Hillside Home School that he had designed for his aunts Nell and Jane Lloyd Jones.

The property that Mrs. Wright turned over to her son had many desirable features. A stream ran through it that was later dammed to form ornamental ponds. In the distance was the Wisconsin River, overlooked by trees, pastures, trails and meadows.

The house closely followed the crest of the hill and was built of native materials, including fieldstone and timber, with low, cedar-shingled roofs. The plan for the Wisconsin house and studio was fluid and

BELOW: *Even in its earliest incarnation, the garden of Taliesin, with integral sculpture and low walls built of native stone, seemed to be a natural part of the landscape.*

PAGES 86-87: *Wright continued to work on Taliesin throughout his life, trying out new designs and methods of building.*

informal, with rooms opening directly onto flagstone terraces at ground level and balconies that framed idyllic views of the countryside. A stone reservoir at the top of the hill provided water to the house, gardens and outbuildings by gravity.

The original complex consisted of a studio in the center, living quarters for draftsmen and workmen on one side, and the main house on the other. After the house was destroyed by arson in 1914, it was rebuilt and additions made to the studio and adjacent areas as well.

As with all Wright's homes and studios, Taliesin was in a constant process of building and rebuilding, apart from the two fires it sustained (the second, in 1925, was caused by an electrical storm.). As at Oak Park, Taliesin served as a laboratory for Wright's experiments in architecture, evolving into a luxurious residence of the Usonian type, built largely on credit, like so many projects that Wright undertook. His appreciation for beautiful things often outpaced his income and landed him deeply in debt.

Over the years, Taliesin became one of the best known and most-visited residences in the United States. During the 1930s, members of the Taliesin Fellowship improved the property and tended to its working farm, vegetable gardens and ornamental plantings. Eventually, the complex took in the former Hillside Home School, with its romantic but enduring Romeo and Juliet windmill, and half a dozen other properties that had long been held by the Lloyd Jones family.

TOP LEFT: *The living room of Taliesin, in 1925, reveals Wright's interest in Oriental art.*

ABOVE LEFT: *Wright framed the view from Taliesin with the heavy stone columns on the terrace.*

LEFT: *Now over 80 years old, the stone walls and paths of Taliesin still seem extremely contemporary.*

Midway Gardens, 1913

(demolished 1929)

Chicago, Illinois

The Midway Gardens project began in exuberance and ended ingloriously some 16 years later, when the grandiose structure was demolished in the wake of Prohibition. It was the brainchild of Wright's friend and client E. C. Waller, Jr., who sought his help in designing a great open-air restaurant and entertainment center just off Chicago's Midway, at Cottage Grove Avenue and 60th Street. The scheme appealed to Wright, who saw the proposed Midway Gardens as more than a mere European-style beer garden. It was to be a year-round attraction, to include a winter garden, an indoor dance floor, and a bar, with ample space for cultural events.

Waller and several other backers raised a portion of the $350,000 budget, while Wright designed the whole complex in a matter of days. Paul Mueller, the engineer who had worked with Wright at Adler & Sullivan and served as contractor for the Larkin Building, was put in charge of the project. Long-time associates like Richard Bock and Alfonso Iannelli provided designs for ornamental works, including abstract sculptures. John Lloyd Wright painted murals and turned his hand to whatever needed doing. Now 20 years old, he would be working with his father on many projects to come. No one involved seemed troubled by the fact that New York architect Stanford White had come to financial grief with a similar complex for the Empire City: Madison Square Garden. Like Wright's Midwestern pleasure dome, the Garden never paid its way.

Lack of working capital probably exacerbated the tensions that arose along with the brick and patterned-concrete walls of the castlelike complex. Inside was a huge, multi-level open space with a stage at one end, overhung by an elaborate acoustic shell. Weird angular finials surmounted the pylons on the upper terraces. Quarrels broke out among the various creative temperaments involved. As Wright recalled in 1936, for the *Architect's Journal* of London, "In the Midway Gardens . . . I tried to complete the synthesis: planting, furnishings, music, painting, and sculpture, all to be one. But I found that musicians, painters, and sculptors were unable to rise to any such synthesis. Only in a grudging and dim way did most of them even understand it as an idea."

Unfortunately, Midway Gardens ran at a loss for only two years before it was sold to a Chicago brewer, who planned to turn it into a conventional beer garden. Prohibition put an end to that use, and the complex was finally razed in 1929.

Sherman M. Booth House, 1915
Glencoe, Illinois

The Sherman M. Booth House is one of several designed for the real-estate development in Glencoe called Ravine Bluffs. Booth was an attorney and a friend of Wright's, who first approached him in 1911 with the commission for a sizable house. The proposed site was a triangular eminence with three steep ravines falling away from it, and Wright was inspired to place the main house on this rising ground with access by a concrete bridge spanning the ravine adjacent to the public street. One wing of the house was to contain utility and servants' rooms on the ground level and a dining room, dining porch, pantry and kitchen on the second floor. Other tile-roofed two-level wings were designed to house bedrooms, baths and sleeping porches. The main block had a music room and a two-story-high living room, which

obviated the problem of lack of natural light that plagued many Wright designs of this period.

In the event, the Booth House as built was not so grand as its original plans, which considerably exceeded the attorney's budget. An ample but more modest house was constructed on part of the land Booth owned in Glencoe. Wright then designed several other houses that Booth built as a real-estate speculation on adjacent land, including the Perry House. Wright did not supervise the construction of the houses in Ravine Bluffs. By 1915 he was deeply involved in plans for construction of the Imperial Hotel in Tokyo – his largest commission to that date and one that necessitated frequent and lengthy trips to Japan.

LEFT: *Wright's use of individual wings for different functions is evident in the Booth House.*

BELOW: *The open plan living room was a Wright innovation.*

RIGHT: *The forecourt of the Imperial Hotel shortly before demolition. Certain decorative elements typical of Wright's American buildings can be found here, and do not look out of place.*

Imperial Hotel, 1915-22
(demolished 1968)

Tokyo, Japan

By 1913 Wright had been collecting Japanese prints for some years and was already an authority on them. On a trip to Japan that year, representatives of the government approached him about designing a grand hotel to replace the aging, German-built Imperial Hotel in Tokyo. Wright was much struck with the possibilities of a project on such a major scale, and he was in desperate need of the $300,000 fee involved. When he returned to the United States, the hotel began to take shape on his drawing board. He also designed a temporary annex to the old hotel, to be used while the main building was under construction. In December 1916, he sailed for Tokyo with his companion Miriam Noel and took up residence in the annex for much of the next seven years.

Frequent earthquakes in the Japanese islands made it necessary to do extensive groundwork before the first brick was laid. The hotel was to occupy a full city block, and there were 60 to 70 feet of mud below the shallow surface soil. The hotel's underpinning consisted of pile-driven concrete pins, closely spaced, that would allow the building to withstand the waves of quake movements. The outer walls – brick reinforced with concrete and steel – were thick and massive at the base and grew thinner toward the top to keep the center of gravity low. The roof was of copper, rather than the customary tile, because of its lighter weight. Western construction techniques were united with Eastern aesthetics in the structure, which did, in fact, survive the record-shattering earthquake that rocked Tokyo and Yokohama in 1923.

The Imperial Hotel was laid out on an axial plan, with guest rooms in the two wings and public rooms in the central area. There was a large reflecting pool before the main entrance and a cavernous multi-level lobby that some guests found overpowering. It was built of brick and carved lava stone (oya) and heavy with bronze urns.

The entire structure was ornate and intricately detailed, and it became even more so over the years that Wright worked on it. He had to please not only the Japanese, who were funding the project, but the foreign visitors they wanted to entertain and impress.

The original Imperial Hotel burned down before its replacement was finished, which put time constraints on a project that resisted rapid completion. Wright's son John spent some time in Tokyo working on the hotel, but he was eventually sent back to the United States, closely followed by Wright's draftsman, Antonin Raymond, who wearied of his employer's frequent outbursts of temper. Finally, Wright himself left Tokyo in 1921, before the hotel was finished. Nevertheless, it remained one of his greatest architectural feats, despite its demolition in 1968, to make way for still another grand hotel. (The entrance lobby was moved to Nagoya.) In this massive undertaking, Wright had produced more than 700 drawings for the building and all its features: furniture, sculpture, murals, tableware, linen, silver, glass, upholstery fabrics and carpets – more than 1,200 of them, including small pieces sewn together to encircle columns and piers. All the carpets were custom woven in China to Wright's specifications. The sheer magnitude of the task makes it seem remarkable that the Imperial Hotel was completed in only eight years – with many other commissions carried out at the same time.

LEFT: *The entrance of the hotel, with its ornamental pool, was reconstructed in Meiji Mura Park near Nagoya in Japan.*

PAGE 94: *The interior of the rebuilt lobby at Meiji Mura Park.*

PAGE 95 TOP: *The Imperial Hotel was built around a series of interior garden courtyards.*

PAGE 95 BOTTOM: *Wright's decoration for the original lobby included painted murals above the fireplaces.*

Hollyhock House (Aline Barnsdall House), 1917

Los Angeles, California

The Barnsdall House on Olive Hill was Wright's second essay in a dwelling for southern California, where he would do extensive work during the 1920s and maintain an office in Los Angeles. He rejected the prevailing Spanish Mission and bungalow styles and took his own architectural route into the Southwest's pre-Columbian past. Unfortunately, the Barnsdall project was compromised by the architect's long absences in Japan, where he was working on the Imperial Hotel, and by the vicissitudes of his relationship with the client, Aline Barnsdall, who was an actress and a wealthy patroness of the arts with decided ideas on how things should be done.

The house was originally intended to be a poured-concrete structure on a grand scale in the line of the Unity Temple design. Eventually, the construction materials were changed to wood frame and cement plaster, although the identifying hollyhock sculptures and finials were executed in poured concrete. The region's mild climate made it possible to include rooftop terraces in the design, which centered around a very large patio court with lawns, pools and fountains. However, as the house had few windows, and those ill placed, there were no views except from terraces and rooftops.

Barnsdall also asked Wright to design a

theater for the property, and several other buildings that would have formed a large complex for the dramatic arts, but these projects were never carried beyond the planning stage.

The Hollyhock House represents a near total departure from Wright's work in the Prairie House style. Its massive, closed volumes give it the look of a brooding Mayan temple, imposed heavily on the surrounding landscape. The roof is rigid and continuous, and the interior spaces are interlocked in a tight grid rather than free-flowing. Features abstracted from nature, like the concrete flowers, have lost their naturalness in the translation into harsh

overbearing images that create distance instead of attraction. In fact, the house much resembles a fortress designed to protect the privacy of a wealthy aristocrat, rather than the centerpiece of a liberal artistic community, which it was intended to be.

ABOVE: *The Barnsdall House reflects Wright's interest in pre-Columbian design.*

PAGE 98 TOP: *The doors and windows of the Barnsdall House are set well back in their frames to shield the rooms from the bright California sun.*

PAGE 98 BOTTOM: *The motif of stylized hollyhocks in cast concrete is a unifying design for the building.*

98 HOLLYHOCK HOUSE (ALINE BARNSDALL HOUSE)

Alice Madison Millard House
(*La Miniatura*), 1923
Pasadena, California

The early 1920s, when Wright was working in California after his return from Japan, saw major innovations. Foremost among them was the introduction of a new building material. which Wright called the textile block. This was a glorified version of the familiar precast concrete block that had long been the ugly stepchild of the construction industry. In Wright's refashioning, the blocks were impressed with decorative patterns by pouring the concrete into molds in which steel or wooden grids formed designs on one or both sides. The blocks were then "woven together" with steel rods running horizontally and vertically inside their hollow grooves.

The first, and most impressive, application of this new technique was in the Alice Madison Millard House. called "La Miniatura," built in a wooded ravine in Pasadena. Mrs. Millard was a widow who had lived in a house designed by Wright in Highland Park, Illinois, during her marriage. She agreed at once to Wright's proposal of the new textile-block construc-

tion, and the small, delightful structure took shape under the eucalyptus trees that shaded the property, rising gracefully to a height of three stories, with terraces at four levels. The two-story-high living room has a mezzanine suspended above the chimney breast and French doors opening onto a cantilevered balcony. The exterior pattern of crosses piercing the blocks filters the sunlight into the well-proportioned rooms. The construction technique allows interior and exterior to be treated in the same manner, comprising a harmonious, richly ornamented whole. A reflecting pool gives back the picture, enhanced by the luxuriant plants of the setting.

Mrs. Millard was extremely happy with the house, which has been occupied continuously for more than 60 years. Eventually, Lloyd Wright doubled the size of the garage designed by his father and added a small studio without impairing the perfect scale of the project. As for Wright, he reported in his autobiography: "I would rather have built this little house than St. Peter's in Rome."

ABOVE: *"La Miniatura" was the first of Wright's textile-block houses.*

Charles Ennis House, 1923

Los Angeles, California

Wright had foreseen the impact of the machine age on architecture even before he delivered his famous lecture on The Art and Craft of the Machine at Hull House in 1901. But it would be more than 20 years before he put entire buildings together from prefabricated, mass-produced modules like the textile blocks of the 1920s. Characteristically, Wright took the new technique to the limit before he turned his attention to the experiments in concrete cantilevers of the 1930s.

The Ennis House is the largest of the four concrete-block houses built in Southern California in 1924. The site – a steep hillside – posed a challenge that was not resolved successfully, as the sheer mass of the outside walls overpowers both the site and the viewer. In addition, long sections of the lower retaining wall on the south side have bulged over time, resisting every effort at improvement.

As conceived by Wright for his wealthy client in 1923, the house comprises a large living room, dining room, family and guest bedrooms, and a series of terraces, steps and stairs to the various levels. The high-ceilinged interior has the look of a Hollywood set for an epic film. Patterned and plain concrete blocks alternate on the forbidding Mayan exterior, unsoftened by the vines and other trailing plants that help to humanize this kind of building.

As with the Barnsdall House, Wright's extended absences from the scene – in this case, at Taliesin – led to deep divisions between architect and client that could not be resolved by Lloyd Wright, who had the misfortune to act as go-between, with major responsibility and no real authority to carry it out. Before the dust of acrimony settled, the Ennises had gone their own way to finish the house without Wright's approval. Teak, marble and bronze predominated within the imposing structure, and the house changed hands many times as new owners tried to cope with the unwieldy and expensive legacy they had acquired. Years later, Wright admitted that the Ennis House design had been too large for the textile-block building method and contrasted it unfavorably with the smaller, relatively more domestic-looking Storer House, built that same year on Hollywood Boulevard.

Built on a ridge in Los Angeles, the massive Ennis House is the most monumental of the textile-block houses.

John Storer House, 1924

Los Angeles, California

The hillside site of the Storer House is not so steep as that of the larger Ennis House. The two-story textile-block structure rises from a terrace supported on a wall of concrete blocks whose severity has been softened by decades of plant growth. Entrance to the central portion of the house is through adjacent French doors that lead into the combined reception hall-dining room. Above these doors a series of tall windows lights the high-ceilinged living room.

The house has a flat roof and two wings, one containing family bedrooms and baths, the other, the kitchen, a servant's bedroom and a bath. There is a semi-detached garage approached by a driveway on this side of the house. As happened frequently on a Wright project, cost overruns became a serious problem for the client, a Los Angeles dentist, and there were many disputes like those that marred the Ennis relationship. Absenteeism on Wright's part – again, he was mainly at Taliesin – left his son Lloyd Wright in charge of supervising the construction.

The Storer House employs three types of concrete blocks: plain, patterned and pierced. The facade has a pleasing symmetry, and the house has worn well, although it must have been a peculiar sight as it took form in the rural area that was

Hollywood in the 1920s. Wright was so eager to see his textile-block building plans materialize that he rashly offered to pay a percentage of the cost by which the house exceeded its budget. (This was also true of the Freeman House.) However, by the 1950s, Wright could look back on the Storer project with equanimity, recalling, "It's a little palace; it looked like a little Venetian palazzo." By the early 1990s, the house had been fully renovated and restored.

ABOVE: *The multi-level Storer House incorporates several textile-block designs in its facade.*

Arizona Biltmore Hotel, 1927

Phoenix, Arizona

Wright's involvement with the design of the luxurious Arizona Biltmore Hotel began with a letter from architect Albert McArthur, who had worked as a draftsman at the Oak Park studio early in his career. His father, Chicago businessman Warren McArthur, had been a friend and client of Wright's, and his two brothers were involved in plans for the hotel, which was to attract wealthy Easterners to Phoenix during the winter months, like Florida and California.

Wright agreed to act as a consultant for the hotel and traveled to Phoenix with his companion, Olgivanna Milanov, and their two children. He was to advise the McArthurs on the use of concrete textile-block construction like that used for the 11 houses designed for California clients by himself and his son, architect Lloyd Wright. The extent of Wright's contribution to the Arizona Biltmore is still debated, but the evidence suggests that it was substantial. The four-story, steel-reinforced main building is constructed of alternating plain and deeply patterned

ABOVE: *Outlying wings duplicate the peaked roof of the main building of the Arizona Biltmore.*

LEFT: *Covered walkways connect the wings of the hotel to the central core.*

concrete blocks whose texture gives the facade its luxurious look. The wide overhang of the peaked roof on one side of the building is pierced in a diagonal pattern to provide both light and shadow in a manner reminiscent of many Prairie House designs. The lobby is very much like that of the Imperial Hotel, on a smaller scale, with a mezzanine above the registry desk and a handling of spatial volumes and ornamentation that bears Wright's signature. Of particular interest is the rich, many-colored glass mural adapted by Wright from a design for *Liberty* magazine that had never been published. It abstracts the forms and colors of desert flora, including the saguaro cactus, which figured in many projects for the Southwest.

In *Many Masks*, Brendan Gill points out that it is in the guest cottages on the grounds that one sees Wright's handiwork most clearly. He writes: "The cottages are ravishing little cubes, themselves composed of cubelike concrete blocks, whose patterns are molded in depth to accept and refract the brilliant Arizona sunlight. They remind us immediately of La Miniatura in being toylike and yet ample – palaces playfully so reduced in scale as to strike us at first glance as being scarcely larger than

dolls' houses. Surely the occupants, whoever they may be when not on holiday, are here but grown-up children, without a care in the world."

The element of playfulness and fantasy would become more pronounced in Wright's work as he grew older, culminating in such designs as the Garden of Eden project for Baghdad and the Manhattan Sports Pavilion design of the 1950s.

ABOVE: *The lobby decoration includes a glass mural of saguaro cactus, and lighted blocks set in concrete piers.*

OPPOSITE: *The dining room, with its tile ceiling, is lit by Wright's original square lamps and the tall windows that run the height of the room.*

ABOVE: *Common elements of Wright's design, including a porte-cochere, casement windows and wide eaves, are still evident at Graycliff.*

RIGHT: *The fireplace and hearth are the focal point of the living room at Graycliff.*

Darwin D. Martin Summer House (Graycliff), 1927

Derby, New York

One of the many commissions undertaken for members and friends of the Darwin D. Martin family is this substantial vacation house on Lake Erie, not far from the Martins' permanent home in Buffalo, New York. It was designed more than 20 years after the house in Buffalo, which Wright worked on in conjunction with the Larkin Company Administration Building.

The building site for Graycliff was a high bluff overlooking the lake, and the house resembles many of those built for wealthy suburban clients in the Midwest. Wright did not supervise the construction or design the furniture and fixtures, apart from the fireplace, closets and so forth. Mrs. Martin had many suggestions to make, as she had for the main house in Buffalo, and Wright was not always amenable to them. The project was marred by delayed schedules and incessant revisions to the plans. The final result was an unusually conventional house – for Wright – with spacious rooms, ample light and informal, comfortable furniture. Most of the client's suggestions were adopted, over Wright's objections, which compromised the design and made Graycliff a less satisfactory house than, say, the William E. Martin House, for Darwin Martin's brother, in Oak Park, Illinois.

108 RICHARD LLOYD JONES HOUSE (WESTHOPE)

Richard Lloyd Jones House (Westhope), 1929

Tulsa, Oklahoma

The concrete-block house that Wright designed for his cousin Richard Lloyd Jones in 1929 was of a different kind than those he had done in Southern California. The design evolved in part from a project that was never realized, due to the stock-market crash of 1929: a small wood-frame and cement-stucco house for a typical city block in Chandler, Arizona, where Wright was working on plans for San Marcos-in-the-Desert. When that project, too, collapsed for lack of funds, Wright returned to Taliesin, where he received the commission from his cousin Richard, a successful newspaper publisher in Tulsa.

The Richard Lloyd Jones House, called Westhope, is atypical of anything else Wright built. It is extremely large, constructed of alternating vertical members of concrete block and glass which make it appear very tall, although it is only two stories high. The house is flat-roofed except at the end of either wing, where glass enclosures extend upward and outward to serve as conservatories for indoor plants, including trees. The concrete block used for the house was unadorned, giving the building a utilitarian appearance rather than the richly detailed look of the textile-block houses for California. In the original perspective drawing, it looks like an office building, not a residence. In *Many Masks*, Brendan Gill reports that it suffered from a defect found in many of Wright's buildings, especially those of an experimental kind – a leaky roof. Apparently, the Lloyd Jones cousins coped with this problem by placing tubs and jars all over the house when the rains came. Herbert Johnson visited the property when Wright started working on the Johnson Wax Administration Building and found it admirable, leaks notwithstanding, which was fortunate, as his own building would have the same problem.

The interior of the Richard Lloyd Jones House recalls the Prairie House style and anticipates the Usonian in its open floor plan, with one area flowing into another. In addition to the usual family rooms, the house has six bedrooms, a library and a recreation room. Wright described it in the 1931 catalog for a European exhibit of his works as "The dwelling house without walls. The palisades with steel sash and glass between substituted. The interior space robed with textiles and light modified by movable screens – both features of the architecture."

Malcolm E. Willey House, 1933

Minneapolis, Minnesota

The design – and redesign – of the Willey House was affected by the Depression, which modified the original plan from two stories to one and got rid of excessive ground-floor space that had been largely wasted in many of the big houses for wealthy suburban clients of former years. In this respect, the Willey House, like the Tulsa residence for Wright's cousin Richard, was transitional between the Prairie House and Usonian styles. Changes in living style, including the near-disappearance of domestic help; smaller families; higher costs; and a general informality in domestic life as compared to previous generations all played a part in the move toward smaller houses and greater economies in the building process.

Wright had always professed a concern for moderate-cost housing for the average American family, and as early as 1915, he had begun work on a series of largely prefabricated houses called the American Readi-Cut System. In essence, much of the work was done at the factory rather than the building site. The lumber was precut and keyed for assembly on the site to effect

a substantial reduction in the cost of skilled labor by the building trades. Over a two-year period, more than 900 drawings of various designs and sizes were produced, and prototypes were built on several Midwestern sites. The same type of systems-built construction was involved in the textile-block and concrete/glass houses of the 1920s.

The Willey House has, among other innovations, a cantilevered upper deck enclosed by a ship-lapped wooden parapet that would reappear often in Wright's future designs, including those for the Sturges and Pauson houses, built in California and Arizona, respectively, in the late 1930s.

ABOVE: *The single-story Willey House is considered a major link between the Prairie style and the Usonian house.*

OPPOSITE: *One of Wright's first designs for a city of the future was built only as a model at Taliesin.*

Broadacre City Model for the Industrial Arts Exhibition at Rockefeller Center, 1935
New York City

Wright's Utopian approach to city planning found its first major expression in the 12-foot-by-12-foot model of what he called "Broadacre City." The scale model comprised a four-square-mile tract of the ideal city Wright had long envisaged. The concept was anticipated in his 1932 book *The Disappearing City*, which sounded the alarm on urban crowding and pollution. Its theme was decentralization. Wright proposed to move the congested, dehumanizing inner city out into the landscape, where it would be reorganized, scaled down and beautified without losing its identity as a center of commerce and culture.

Since his years with Louis Sullivan, Wright had recognized that the skyscraper was the characteristic form of future cities. What he objected to most strongly was crowding such high-rise buildings together, as in Manhattan, so that they shut out light and air and diminished their

occupants. He advocated a parklike setting for each skyscraper, and a new kind of construction that would eliminate the clifflike masses of stone on steel post-and-beam armatures that dominated the urban landscape across the nation.

Innovative Wrightian solutions to the problem included such designs as the 1929 project for the National Life Insurance Building in Chicago – essentially a reinforced-concrete slab structure in which all the supports were centrally located, with screen walls of glass and stamped metal. The client backed away from the project because the design was so unusual, and it went into the Wright archives as one of those designs that he could later "shake out of his sleeve," as he put it, and execute for a more discerning client. This design reappeared later in the evolving concept of Broadacre City, along with other imaginative high-rise projects like Crystal Heights

for Washington, D.C. (1939) and the Mile High Illinois Building for Chicago (1956).

In the model constructed by the apprentices at Taliesin North and Ocotillo Camp, in Arizona, Wright realized his new noncity in miniature, complete with bridges, overpasses, service stations, parks and houses, widely spaced in a hilly landscape. He first updated the concept in the 1945 book *When Democracy Builds* and again in *The Living City*, published in 1958, a year before his death. The original model was displayed in several major American cities after the 1935 exhibition at New York City's Rockefeller Center. It can now be seen at Taliesin North.

Despite the insurmountable difficulties of implementing such a concept, Wright's vision of the decentralized city provoked lively debate and engendered lasting ideas among urban planners, architects and average citizens alike.

Herbert Jacobs House (I), 1936

Madison, Wisconsin

The 1930s brought not only major commissions, but new concepts that Wright would explore and expand upon for the rest of his working life. Despite the Depression, the community formed at Taliesin in 1932 was fully occupied with such projects as Broadacre City; the Edgar J. Kaufmann, Sr., House, Fallingwater; and the Johnson Wax Company Administration Building in

Racine, Wisconsin. Another Wisconsin project with far-reaching implications was the small Usonian house designed for journalist Herbert Jacobs and his wife Katherine in 1936. This was the prototype for scores of Wright (and "Wrightian") houses to be built all over the country in the decades to come.

As originally conceived, the Usonian

house was to be a moderately priced, partially prefabricated structure of wood, glass and brick construction with a flat roof. The Jacobs House (much of which was built by the clients themselves) was budgeted at $4,500 and comprises only 1,500 square feet of space in an L-shaped single story. Heating coils were embedded in gravel after ground preparation and

*In a series of photographs taken upon
completion of construction in 1940, the
Jacobs House is seen from the private
garden side (Opposite, top and bottom).
Inside, the brick and wooden walls of the
dining room (top) and living room
(bottom) are decorative as well as part of
the construction.*

covered by a concrete floor slab. Brick wall masses carry most of the roof supports, and the remaining walls are prefabricated of wood and plywood, laminated with insulating paper between them, the "sandwich" being screwed together. The roof framing utilizes laminated two-by-four boards in three offsets, rather than the more expensive two-by-twelve-foot lumber construction. Floor-to-ceiling French doors open onto an inviting view of garden and slope behind the house, while the facade presented to the street is essentially featureless except for clerestory windows high on the outside wall. The traditional dining room was eliminated. Instead, an informal dining area was juxtaposed to the kitchen. It would be variously called a dinette or a living kitchen: the idea was an informal gathering place for family and friends that assumed housewife and cook were one and the same person. From the kitchen/dining area, the living room extends in one direction, and the bedrooms extend in another. The garage was replaced by a carport. The house itself Wright called Usonia One.

Fallingwater (Edgar J. Kaufmann, Sr., House), 1936
Mill Run, Pennsylvania

Fallingwater is widely considered Wright's architectural masterpiece, and is one of the best-known private houses in the world. It is the fullest realization of his lifelong ideal of a living place completely at one with nature. Constructed on three levels primarily of reinforced concrete, sandstone and glass, its soaring cantilevered balconies anchored in solid rock, the house appears to float in space above the waterfall in its wooded glen. It is intimately related to the rock ledges, trees and rushing streams of the western Pennsylvania site the Kaufmanns had long used as a weekend retreat from their Pittsburgh home and business.

The cantilevered planes of the house are held together by rough sandstone walls of varying thickness, quarried nearby and laid in alternating courses. The southern exposure, facing the view of the stream, has walls made primarily of glass. One particularly arresting feature is the vertical shaft of mitered glass that merges with stone and steel on that side of the house. Wild rhododendrons add year-round beauty to the natural setting.

Most of Fallingwater's floor space is devoted to the massive, stone-flagged living room and the terraces and canopy-slabs that soar out in four directions. The three bedrooms, kitchen and utility areas take up only a small proportion of the house. In 1939 a guest house, with garage and servants' quarters, was added to the complex on a slope above the main house. It is reached by a winding covered walkway that makes ingenious use of curved and geometric concrete forms. Similar forms encircle some of the trees in the garden, linking house and setting like graceful ribbons.

The Kaufmanns were understandably delighted with their Appalachian retreat, which they had originally envisioned as a kind of rustic lodge where they could "rough it" in relative comfort. Instead, they found themselves the owners – and virtual curators – of what is probably the best-known private house in the United States and a landmark of international architecture. But the family didn't allow this to affect their genuine enjoyment of Fallingwater, or their lifelong friendship with the architect. Edgar J. Kaufmann, Jr., who was an apprentice at Taliesin before he brought his father and Wright together for the project, wrote a book about the house, entitled *Fallingwater*. He stated therein that "My father was no monarch and his house was not conceived as a public monument." The fact that it became one did not detract from its original function as a much-loved and well-used home.

LEFT: *A flight of stairs runs from the living room to the level of the water just above the falls.*

OPPOSITE: *Wright's use of cantilever construction is most apparent at Fallingwater.*

116 FALLINGWATER (EDGAR J. KAUFMANN, SR., HOUSE)

OPPOSITE TOP: *Wright built the house around the projecting rocks which form part of the hearth.*

OPPOSITE BOTTOM: *The guest house living room features a built-in window seat and bookshelves.*

RIGHT: *A covered walkway connects the main house to the guest house above and creates a series of levels seen through the surrounding trees.*

Honeycomb House (Paul R. Hanna House), 1936

Palo Alto, California

One of the most distinguished and innovative residences of Wright's career was the Paul R. Hanna House, called the Honeycomb House for its hexagonal design units. The clients, Paul and Jean Hanna, were young members of the academic community who had followed Wright's work since the early 1930s and visited Taliesin several times. When Paul Hanna accepted a position on the faculty of Stanford University in 1935, the couple asked Wright to design a house for them and their three young chilren. The building site chosen was on a hillside overlooking the campus, and the Hannas worked closely with Wright on the innovative design for their house.

The primary construction materials were brick, copper and glass. The hexagonal module called for contrasting high and low ceilings in every room and caused confusion among the building tradespeople involved, who had to deal with 120-degree angles instead of the customary 90-degree right angle of rectangular room designs. After ground preparation, precast hexago-

nal tiles were laid down on concrete and the walls were erected on the intersection lines. Sections of glass doors in the living room and playroom were designed to fold away to the sides, opening the rooms fully to extensive outdoor terraces that took advantage of the region's mild climate. Redwood added warmth to the interior walls, and every piece of furniture and detailing was specially designed by Wright to fit the hexagonal plan. The result was a dwelling of great beauty and utility, which thousands of people have visited over the years, and which served as a prototype for dozens of other houses based on the same unit system.

During the 1950s, Wright made extensive changes based on the family's changing needs with the departure of grown children. A guesthouse and workshop were added and the interior was remodeled to provide fewer but larger rooms. The garden is especially beautiful, with its broad stone steps, where jets of water play, and a carved lava-stone urn, two tons in weight, from the Imperial Hotel. Professor Hanna

had it shipped from Tokyo before the grand structure was demolished in 1968.

In 1974 the Hannas deeded the house to Stanford University, and the Nissan Motor Company contributed half a million dollars to its endowment three years later as a gesture of appreciation for Wright's life-long interest in Japanese culture.

S. C. Johnson & Son
Administration Building, 1936
Racine, Wisconsin

The intensely creative period of the 1930s resulted in one of Wright's best-known buildings – a milestone in commercial architecture. He undertook the complex (a Research Tower was added in 1944) for Herbert F. Johnson, president of the Johnson Wax Company, who admired his work and agreed with Wright's intention to make the building "as inspiring a place to work in as any cathedral was in which to worship."

When Wright first visited the site, in Racine's industrial district. he urged Johnson to move the whole plant out into the country and build a model town for employees around it. The constraints of the $200,000 budget, and the Depression, made this plan impractical, so the architect concentrated on creating a "sealed" environment like that of the Larkin Building in Buffalo (but without the forbidding monolithic look of the earlier structure). "Streamlined" was the word Wright used often in referring to the Johnson Administration Building, and streamlined it was. Light came in from above, via skylights and a clerestory band below the cornice.

The principal building supports were dendriform (mushroom-shaped) columns, slender at the base and increasing in thickness as they rise to form the ceiling with their petal-shaped terminals. The columns were made of hollow reinforced concrete, while ordinary glass was replaced by Pyrex tubing throughout the building. Such innovations raised doubts on the part of the Wisconsin Industrial Commission, which demanded that Wright build a single column and test-load it with sacks of sand to prove that it could support the specified weight. With the help of his son-in-law, engineer Wesley Peters, and Mendel Glickman, who had helped construct Fallingwater, the Kaufmann House on Bear Run, Wright put the requisite test column in place. It proved to support 60 tons of sand and iron – five times the required capacity. Johnson and his staff were exultant, and the building proceeded. (As it turned out, the Pyrex tubing of the skylights and covered walkways was not watertight, an ongoing problem that was finally solved by building a conventional skylit roof over the original one.)

The cleanliness and light of the work area were an immediate success with Johnson's employees. He claimed that people who had turned him down before the building opened now came in and asked for jobs. Fortunately, the privately owned business was a wealthy one, as the cost of

construction came in at close to three million dollars, spread out over a three-year period. Wright also designed all the office furniture for the building, most of it in metal, to harmonize with the soft rust red of the interiors and the streamlined quality of the environment.

The building opened in 1939 to instant acclaim and soon became a landmark of international architecture. It has since been earmarked for preservation by the AIA. Manfredo Tafuri and Francesco Dal Co, authors of the book *Modern Architecture*, wrote of it: "The Johnson Wax Company administration building is a perfect prolongation of the organic utopia of Broadacre City. A monument to the work of the Usonian, it no longer presupposes the dialectical clash with the city that even the St. Mark's Tower still professed. Its various elements emerge fluidly and without breaks from the enveloping forms of the buildings."

ABOVE: *The core of the Research Tower, from which the building is hung, is visible at twilight.*

OPPOSITE TOP: *The great workroom at Johnson Wax is divided only by dendriform columns.*

OPPOSITE BOTTOM: *The steel and wooden desks designed for the Johnson Wax Office are still in use.*

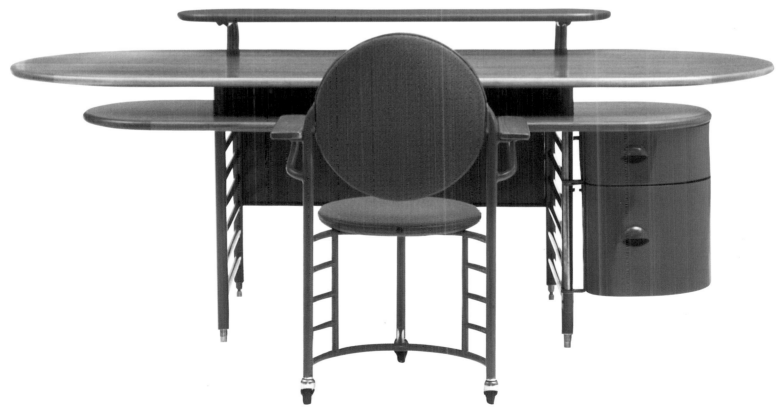

Taliesin West, 1937-59
Scottsdale, Arizona

Wright's long love affair with the South-western desert began in 1927, when he was invited to help build the Arizona Biltmore Hotel in Phoenix as a consultant to the architect, Albert Chase McArthur. As a result of that project, Wright met the entrepreneur Alexander Chandler, who had given his name to a town near Phoenix where he had built a resort hotel. Chandler proposed to build a much larger resort to be called San Marcos-in-the-Desert, and Wright began work on the plans in 1928. That winter he left Wisconsin with seven draftsmen and his family and set up Ocotillo Camp in the desert near Chandler. This hand-built, board-and-canvas complex on wooden frames was the prototype for Taliesin West, which was begun 10 years later, long after the San Marcos project came to grief in the stock-market crash of 1929.

The site for Taliesin West was the desert around Scottsdale, and, like its predecessor, it was built entirely by Wright and his apprentices from Taliesin North. From 1938 onward, members of the Fellowship would accompany him to Arizona for the winter months, adding to, enlarging and revising the new complex for the next 22 years. But its basic form remained constant: massive base walls of desert masonry, surmounted by redwood frames and tentlike white canvas, like a sailing ship. The diffused light that came through the canvas softened the harsh glare of the sun and provided an ideal environment for both studio and living quarters.

Strong diagonal slashes break the long straight axis of the complex, which is as one with its desert setting. Multicolored stone from the site was mixed with the concrete that forms its base walls and terraces. They contrast strikingly with the richly appointed interiors, with gold pile carpeting, woven textiles, hanging desert plants, native pottery – even a grand piano. Taliesin's living quarters are more like those of a legendary Arabian sheik than those of a rough-and-ready American frontier camp. The tall candelabralike saguaro cactus, an "architectural" plant that Wright cherished, found its reflection in his desert buildings and such organic detailing as the stained-glass mural for the grand lobby of the Arizona Biltmore Hotel. The tension inherent in Wright's lifelong quest for the ultimate synthesis was expressed at Taliesin West as almost nowhere else. Over time, the redwood posts and rafters gave way to steel, and the canvas to glass and plastic, but the timeless quality of the complex remains unchanged. It still houses the Taliesin Fellowship during much of the year.

OPPOSITE: *The drafting room skylights can be covered by canvas shades.*

ABOVE: *The entrance to Taliesin West is masked by a stone pylon and fountain.*

PAGES 124-125: *The sloping walls of the exterior of the drafting room were built of native stone.*

TALIESIN WEST 123

LEFT: *The facade of the south drafting room framed by the mountains near Phoenix.*

OPPOSITE BOTTOM: *The massive sculptural trusses of the drafting room are softened by plantings and shrubbery.*

BELOW: *Members of the Taliesin Fellowship and their families, including Wright and his wife Olgivanna (in striped dress) met each afternoon for tea.*

Herbert F. Johnson House
(Wingspread), 1937
Wind Point, Wisconsin

The focal point of this large, elegant house is a three-story living room resembling a tepee in its conical shape – perhaps a reflection of Wright's perennial interest in ancient American cultures. (He experimented with this shape in several projects, including that for the Lake Tahoe Summer Colony in 1922.)

Four wings extend from the house's central area, one each for the children's quarters, master bedroom suite, guest bedrooms, and kitchen with servants' quarters. Wright compared this "zoned plan" to that of the 1907 house for Avery Coonley in Riverside, Illinois. However, the Johnson House is much larger and occupies a stretch of open country near Lake Michigan, rather than a suburban lot. In fact, Wingspread is one of the very few Wright houses that was actually built on a prairie.

A massive brick chimney core in the high-ceilinged living area has five fireplaces on two levels. It acts as a point of demarcation for the various living spaces, each of which has its own fireplace: entrance hall, living and dining areas, and a mezzanine library. A glass observatory is on the south side of the house, where the chimney emerges from the tiled roof. The roof is pierced by small skylights.

Four large French doors open from the central living area onto gardens, terraces and swimming pool. Wingspread has 14,000 square feet of space, and its towering chimney and immense skylighted living area make it an imposing structure. Since Wright's death, the philanthropic Wingspread Foundation, founded by Herbert Johnson, has occupied the house, which is used as a conference center.

In *Modern Architecture*, published by Harry N. Abrams in 1979, Manfredo Tafuri states that "Not even in the Usonian houses did Wright succeed in expressing himself with equal originality and tension." In fact, Wingspread *is* a Usonian house writ very large.

OPPOSITE: *The roof of the central core, or "wigwam" as Wright called it, is pierced for a series of clerestory windows.*

ABOVE: *The angular swimming pool fits within the wings Wright designated for the use of the children and the servants.*

Solomon R. Guggenheim Museum, 1943-1956

New York City

The planning and construction of the Solomon R. Guggenheim Museum occupied a full 16 years of revisions, delays and disappointments in the latter part of Wright's long career. Before it was over, he had to take an apartment in New York's Plaza Hotel – wryly called Taliesin East – to deal with the ceaseless demands of the project.

The commission came from the wealthy collector of nonobjective art, Solomon R. Guggenheim, who wanted a museum unlike any other. Curator Hilla Rebay was a moving force behind the project, but all parties concerned were frustrated by long delays in implementing it, including the building moratorium imposed by World War II and the difficulty of finding a suitable site in crowded and expensive Manhattan.

The spiral form figured in the design from the earliest stages, in several versions: with each of the tiers the same size, with the tiers growing progressively smaller toward the top, or with the tiers expanding in size as the building rose. The latter choice – that of the expanding spiral – made the best use of the space available while combining structural and spatial principles toward which Wright had worked throughout his 75-year career.

The primary construction medium was concrete, both sprayed and poured in forms, which allowed for plasticity. Inside the building, a shallow-spiraling ramp, of the same curvilinear form as the exterior, conducted the visitor from the topmost tier, reached by elevator, to the bottom of the ramp, viewing the artworks as he progressed. The building was skylit from its domed ceiling, and its central space was occupied by a large open court.

Many artists feared that the unusual shape of the building and the pitch of the ramp would make it impossible to exhibit their works. Similar concerns were expressed by the museum's board of trustees and its director, James Johnson Sweeney.

Curator Hilla Rebay objected to the design on grounds that the building might overpower the works of art. While the museum was under construction Wright prepared a series of interior perspectives, with replications of specific paintings in the collection, to show how the exhibitions would be mounted.

Attached to "the Ziggurat," as Wright called it, was a small office wing called the "Monitor." To increase the museum's gallery space, at Rebay's request, Wright proposed a tall freestanding structure set well behind the main building for permanent display of the collection's masterpieces. He wanted to add a roof garden, but Rebay replied with some asperity that New York was too dirty to make this suggestion practical. Wright's plan to clad the exterior in cream-colored marble was also voted down as too expensive – which it was.

When the museum opened on upper Fifth Avenue in 1959, it elicited a storm of criticism and praise alike. It has remained controversial to this writing, and has recently undergone extensive renovations.

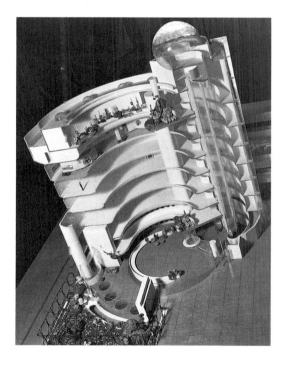

PAGES 130-131: *Wright's "Ziggurat" is still one of the most striking buildings on New York's Fifth Avenue.*

ABOVE LEFT: *The continuous ramp and central court are lit by a skylight in the dome.*

ABOVE RIGHT: *The original half-model of the Guggenheim shows Wright's plan for the roof garden and the clear dome over the elevator shaft.*

Florida Southern College, 1938
Lakeland, Florida

In 1938 Wright was invited to design an entire campus for small, struggling Florida Southern College by its president, Dr. Ludd Spivey. The two men had much in common, and Wright seized the opportunity eagerly, partly because of his lifelong interest in progressive education and partly to implement his ideas on an appropriate educational setting. He believed that contemporary American college students deserved something that hadn't been modeled on outmoded European institutions.

The building site faced a lake bordered by citrus orchards. The site plan was kept to a low scale, except for the vertical thrust of the Annie Pfeiffer Chapel. Its steel tower was designed to serve as a light source for the building, into which daylight would filter through hanging plants in concrete planters. The planters proved unworkable, but the skylighting plan works well. The chapel's interior recalls that of Unity Temple – spare and spacious – and fosters a close connection between speaker and audience.

The master plan for the campus, con-structed mainly of reinforced concrete blocks, brick and steel, called for a series of low white buildings connected by a covered esplanade as shelter from the region's tropical sun and heavy rainfalls in the winter months. Not all the projected buildings were realized. Those that were built included the Minor Chapel, a circular library, the administration building, an Industrial Arts complex, the Pfeiffer Chapel, a home for the Science and Cosmography Department, three seminar buildings, and a water dome (fountain) that never worked properly and was finally filled in. One attractive feature of the campus is the use of textured concrete blocks inset with multicolored glass that refract the Florida sun in a way reminiscent of the more traditional stained-glass windows.

Much of the construction work at Florida Southern was done by the students, who defrayed part of their tuition costs by mixing concrete, making blocks, and pouring concrete floor slabs and walkways. (Perhaps this experience proved especially useful for those who went into the building trades.)

ABOVE: *The Annie Pfeiffer Chapel with its steel tower is the most visible landmark on the Florida Southern campus.*

OPPOSITE: *A concrete pier of one of the covered colonnades is reflected in a garden pool.*

George Sturges House, 1939
Brentwood Heights, California

The comparatively small and compact Sturges House makes striking use of the cantilever principle on a steep hillside that was left largely undisturbed. The rectangular shape of the building grows more compressed as it rises to several levels from the brick-pedestal foundation. The ship-lapped redwood parapet of the terrace is typical of the Usonian style, as is the overhead canopy. It is pierced to admit light to the living room and bedrooms that open onto the terrace through a series of French doors.

Inside the house, the living-dining area adjoins a fireplace mass on one side; the kitchen and bath are on the opposite side. The house is positioned to look out over the treetops. It has a presence that is at once airy and intrinsic to the site.

The Sturges House is a good example of the versatility of the Usonian style, which would be applied in a wide variety of climates and natural settings all over the country. It was this concept that made Wright so widely known and imitated during the last two decades of his long career. In *The Natural House* (1954), he

claimed to have built more than a hundred Usonian homes between 1936 and the publication date of the book. Some disagree that his work of the 1950s should be included in the Usonian category.

ABOVE: *The entrance to the Sturges House brings the visitor onto the second floor above the utility area.*

OPPOSITE: *The cantilever balcony is duplicated by the redwood-framed canopy above.*

Goetsch-Winckler House, 1939
Okemos, Michigan

Alma Goetsch and Katherine Winckler were members of the faculty of Michigan State University in Lansing, where a group of professors commissioned Wright to design seven houses for a projected faculty community in nearby Okemos. The Goetsch-Winckler House was the only one built, due to difficulties with design approval on the part of the local banks, a problem often encountered by Wright because of his innovative plans.

The house is similar in plan to the Sturges House, but the Michigan site is flat and the horizontal planes of the structure are more pronounced. Entry is past the carport and follows a sheltered walk into a gallery off the living room. A drop in the land on this southern end of the site means that the living area overlooks the trees, to pleasing effect. The expansive living area is broadly defined, and the house does not feel constricted despite the fact that interior space is organized into bands: workspace to gallery, chimney/dining area to a side wall, sitting room to glass doors and a view of the walled lawn, and south window bay with planters. There is a clear view from one window-wall to the other.

The simple exterior, with its triple-tiered cantilevered eaves and contrasting brick and glass surfaces, makes this one of the most elegant of the Usonian houses.

The multiple roof lines and angles of the Goetsch-Winckler House eliminate the concept of the house as a box, a concept Wright deplored.

TOP: *The bedroom wing is reached from the living room by the hallway lit by French doors, and is concealed behind the paneled wall.*

ABOVE: *The carport, one of Wright's inventions, has become an integral part of the house.*

OPPOSITE: *The kitchen and the living room are divided by a Wright-designed table whose elements can be moved, extending the table in different directions.*

Gregor Affleck House, 1940

Bloomfield Hills, Michigan

The handsome Gregor Affleck House was built in 1941 for a chemical engineer who had grown up in Spring Green, Wisconsin, shortly after Wright went to Chicago. Affleck was acquainted with the Lloyd Joneses, and he commissioned his Bloomfield Hills, Michigan, house when he was 50 years old.

The house follows an L-plan that conforms closely to its hilly, wooded site. Workspace, services, carport and bedroom are built up on the edge of a ravine spanned by the living area. Entry is through a loggia lighted from above, with an open well overlooking a pool and stream. A boarded terrace with a partial overhang has a view of the pond formed by the stream.

Builder Harold Turner was responsible for the lapped cypress walls and the in-clines formed by the typically Usonian plywood cores. The interior of the house is a study in the skillful use of natural materials. The most striking feature of the Affleck House is its interrelationship to the site on many levels. The high loggia is overlooked by guest-room windows at a higher level. It looks down, in turn, to the 40-foot living room below it. Climbing plants soften the fretted plywood rooflights, and the shady area beneath the house has two seats connected by a bridge from which to view the woods and pond. The interior woodwork has the quality of custom-made cabinetry, thanks to Turner, who worked on many Usonian houses for Wright, including the Hanna, Rebhuhn, Armstrong and Wall houses, built over a six-year period between 1937 and 1941.

OPPOSITE: *The house and cantilever balcony are set upon a brick pier which allows the visitor to walk beneath it.*

ABOVE: *The sun room and living quarters are built on foundations, a half-story higher than the cantilevered living-dining room.*

Herbert Jacobs House (II), 1946
Middleton, Wisconsin

After some years of living in their Usonian house in Madison, Wisconsin, Herbert and Katherine Jacobs returned to Wright for plans for a moderately priced house in the country. The war years put a moratorium on almost all residential construction, but in 1946 the plans for the second Jacobs House could be implemented. The site was a hilltop in the Wisconsin countryside and the objective was a dwelling that would provide more room for the couple and their three growing children. Wright's experimentation with new forms found expression in what he called the solar hemicycle house.

The second Jacobs House was placed several feet below grade in a dug-out garden area, with a south-facing facade made primarily of glass and a solid-earth berm at the rear. The design took account of Wisconsin's hot summers and bone-chilling winters, as a broad roof overhang sheltered the half-circle of family living areas on the ground floor, with bedrooms on a mezzanine above them, that were most exposed to the sun. The earthern berm protected the house from winter winds – a concept similar to that of the sod houses built in the Great Plains states by the pioneers.

The primary construction material was stone, quarried nearby, and the entrance was through a tunnel cut through the berm – a feature that enhanced the sense of privacy and shelter that Wright designed into all his houses. As they had before, the Jacobses did much of the construction work themselves, which effected considerable savings on the cost of the house, which was ready for occupancy by the end of 1948.

ABOVE: *The hemicyclical Jacobs House is set into a hilltop, with windows facing south.*

OPPOSITE: *The pool outside is duplicated inside, behind the wall of glass and French doors which catch the sun.*

Unitarian Church, 1947

Shorewood Hills, Wisconsin

Wright's commissions in ecclesiastical architecture included several Unitarian churches, from Unity Temple in Oak Park to this triangular house of worship in Shorewood Hills, Wisconsin. The norm in such cases was a modest budget, but the Shorewood Hills congregation was determined to have Frank Lloyd Wright design its church, and the aging architect took a deep personal interest in the commission. The site was about 36 miles from Taliesin and Wright spent considerable time there overseeing construction, while the Taliesin Fellowship produced numerous plans for interior detailing.

The plan consists essentially of a large and a smaller triangle adjoined. The sanctuary is in the larger portion, open to the smaller, which is used for social functions and other informal gatherings of the congregation. The low ceiling over this portion of the building rises to the prow-shaped roof over the sanctuary, terminating in a series of glass windows behind the pulpit. The pastor officiates in front of these windows, while the choir is placed on a balcony above him.

The low wings on either sides of the building house the Sunday school and the kitchen facilities, respectively. The copper roof, employed in buildings as diverse as the Imperial Hotel and Florida Southern College, is lightweight and contributes to a sense that the building could take flight at any moment. The effect of the steeply pitched roof that rises to a point has been compared to the appearance of hands joined in prayer. The great windows of the prow originally overlooked the surrounding countryside, with a distant view of Lake Mendota, but the growth of the city has narrowed this perspective. Fortunately, property was secured sufficient to maintain a belt of greenery between the church and adjacent buildings.

The great facade of the Unitarian church has been compared to a ship's prow.

LEFT: *The pipes of the organ can be seen through the great window.*

LEFT BELOW: *The striking copper roof has been carefully angled to deal with the heavy snows of winter in Michigan.*

OPPOSITE: *The choir loft and its canopy are cantilevered over the chancel.*

Usonia Homes Cooperative, 1947

Pleasantville, New York

Wright's abiding interest in moderate-cost cooperative housing was expressed in several projects that were never realized, including a scheme for a worker's cooperative housing project in Detroit (1942). The prototypes for the Usonia Homes Cooperative, in Westchester County, New York, were Parkwyn Village and Galesburg Country Homes, both located near Kalamazoo, Michigan. For both these not-for-profit cooperatives, Wright laid out a ground plan for winding roads through wooded terrain and individual one-acre plots laid out in circles, which Wright called discs. As he described the plan in *Architectural Forum* (January 1948), "No lot line touches another wherever the scheme is perfect. All interspaces are to be planted to some native shrub like barberry or sumach, throwing a network of color in pattern over the entire tract."

The Usonia Homes Cooperative resulted from the energy of a young engineer, David Henken, who had spent a year studying with Wright at Taliesin. He inspired a group of young New Yorkers with moderate incomes to purchase about a hundred acres of woodland in Westchester County, not far from New York City, and asked Wright to map out a system of roads and design several houses for the site. The steep hillsides and rock outcroppings of the tract dictated the plan and grade of the roads, adjoined by the circular plots for which Wright designed three Usonian houses, including the well-known Sol Friedman House. At that point, the project was turned over to local architects. The setting is not dissimilar to that for the Ravine Bluffs development in Glencoe, Illinois, undertaken by Wright as far back as 1915.

LEFT TOP: *The mushroom-shaped carport of the Friedman House. The houses in the private Usonia Cooperative are not accessible to photographers or the public.*

LEFT BOTTOM: *The lower stone cylinder of the Friedman House has windows which alternate square and round bottom frames.*

OPPOSITE TOP: *The circular form of the house is repeated in the carport roof and the wall around the front door.*

OPPOSITE BOTTOM: *The living-dining area in the lower cylinder overlooks the wooded landscape of Westchester County.*

Mrs. Clinton Walker House, 1948
Carmel, California

The setting for the Walker House is a stretch of rocky beach along the Pacific Coast, for which the client required a moderately priced house that took full advantage of its seaside location. The challenging site and the budget constraints resulted in a unique small house that drew upon plans for similar sites that had never been implemented.

The broad roof of the Walker House is supported largely by the mass of a central chimney for the fireplace that Wright considered a near-necessity in domestic architecture. A nearly continuous band of casement windows, designed to open downward rather than outward, overlooked the Pacific. The window alteration allowed air to enter the house freely while excluding blown spray and high winds.

Wright called this project the "Cabin on the Rocks" and, as always, resisted alterations to the design suggested by the client and even her friends. In the end, Mrs. Walker had the house built largely as Wright had designed it, and both were highly pleased with the result. Years later, as documented by Bruce Pfeiffer in his book *Letters to Clients*, Wright visited the house and wrote to Mrs. Walker afterward: "I hope this tiny aristocrat among the Carmel bourgeois, so exciting in itself, is not only a domestic experience giving you the joy you, its progenitor, deserve, but a spiritual uplift." The only defect of the house, as Mrs. Walker saw it, was a problem shared by many of Wright's clients: the fireplace smoked.

RIGHT: *The terrace of the Walker House seems to jut into the Pacific Ocean.*

PAGES 154-155: *The roof of porcelain enamel and copper is cantilevered over the corbelled windows of the hexagonal living room.*

V. C. Morris Gift Shop, 1948

San Francisco, California

The ramped spiral appeared in many projects of the 1940s and 1950s, from the unbuilt Pittsburgh civic center to the Guggenheim Museum in New York City, completed after years of planning and travail in 1959. On a smaller, but most effective scale, the same principle was used for the V. C. Morris Gift Shop in San Francisco, which is widely admired as an architectural breakthrough. Here a small retail establishment takes on unexpected dignity and importance by an ingenious use of materials and spatial volumes.

The outside wall of narrow bricks defines the horizontal elements of the building, while the Romanesque arch of the entryway, edged with four concentric bands of brick, harks back to the monumental Golden Door design produced by Wright and Sullivan for the World's Columbian Exposition in Chicago in 1893.

Light is a major element of the design, from the double row of exterior lights housed in glass bricks and the small rectangular lights at the entryway to the concave coffered ceiling above the helical ramp of the interior. The customer moves up the ramp to view the merchandise in glass enclosures and through circular openings – a process not dissimilar to that devised for viewing the artworks of the Guggenheim Museum. Wright compared the spiral form to an unbroken wave and used it increasingly in such diverse settings as this urban shop in northern California and the Southwestern desert setting of the Phoenix residence for his son David Wright, built in the early 1950s.

David Wright House, 1950

Phoenix, Arizona

The drawings for the circular house that Wright designed for his son David in Phoenix are entitled "How to Live in the Southwest," and the residence is ideally suited to the environment. The site was a large flat tract surrounded by citrus trees that obscured a distant view of Camelback Mountain, and Wright's first objective was to raise the house from ground level to take advantage of this view. (The citrus orchards he referred to as "David's lawn.")

A second advantage of elevating the house – on large concrete piers – was the creation of a shade garden beneath it, through which cooling air could circulate. A wide ramp, partly planted in flower gardens, gave access to the dwelling level and reflects Wright's simultaneous preoccupation with the Guggenheim Museum project, still far from completion.

David Wright was a businessman dealing in concrete blocks, and this was the primary building material. Unlike his brothers John and Lloyd, David was not an architect, but he was familiar with engineering techniques and served as the general contractor for his house. He introduced several elements not included in the original design, including steel reinforcements and braces for the wooden roof. The large spiral ramp that leads to the entrance deck of the cantilevered, single-story structure is succeeded by a second ramp leading to the roof-deck. Wright also designed the furniture for the house, and, several years later, a beautiful rug patterned with circles and curves like those of the house itself.

BELOW: *The lower spiral ramp leads to the living quarters of the David Wright House.*

PAGES 158-159: *The strong circular pattern of the rug is echoed by the ceiling treatment.*

Harold C. Price Company Tower, 1952

Bartlesville, Oklahoma

The seed of the Price Tower was planted in 1929, when Wright designed an innovative high-rise building for the grounds of the historic St.Mark's Church in the Bowery in New York City. This unrealized project for his friend and client William Norman Guthrie utilized what Wright called a "tap-root" foundation system to support and supplement the 22-story building's main core of concrete and steel, which extended deeply into the earth. From this core, can-tilevered floors spread out like the branches of a tree. The plan for Saint Mark's Tower was one of many invitations to re-examine the form and function of the skyscraper that Wright extended over the years, most of which were refused by clients who lacked the funds – or the cour-age – to carry out these designs.

When Harold C. Price, Sr., approached Wright some 23 years later with a request for a low-rise office building for his pipe-line company in Bartlesville, Oklahoma, Wright saw an opportunity to realize the St. Mark's Tower project in the hot flat-lands of the Middle West. He astonished his client by producing a proposal for a high-rise, mixed-use tower with duplex apartments in one quadrant of the build-ing, rental offices on the other three sides, and Price Company offices at the top. However, Price was so taken with the handsome plans for the tower that he effec-tively agreed to go into the real-estate busi-ness as well as the oil business by con-structing the building. The two men compromised on 19 stories instead of 22.

As Wright described the structure in his book *The Story of the Tower*, published by Horizon Press in 1956 with an introduc-tion by Harold Price: "This skyscraper, planned to stand free in an open park and thus be more fit for human occupancy, is as nearly organic as steel in tension and con-crete in compression can make it. . . . A composite shaft of concrete rises through the floors, each slab engaging the floors at 19 levels. Each floor proceeds outward from the shaft as a cantilever slab . . . simi-lar to the branch of a tree from its trunk."

In the course of building the tower, Wright became fast friends with the Price family, who asked him to design two houses for them, one for the senior Prices in Phoenix, and one for Harold Price, Jr. and his family in Bartlesville.

OPPOSITE: *The Price Tower is constructed of reinforced concrete with copper-faced parapets and louvers.*

LEFT: *At night bands of light emphasize the horizontal planes of the building.*

OPPOSITE: *Murals of enameled metal decorate the lobby.*

Harold C. Price, Jr., House
(Hillside), 1953
Bartlesville, Oklahoma

While the Price Tower was under construction in the mid-1950s, Harold Price, Jr., was frequently on the site, expressing his active interest in the project. His brother Joe, who took the photographs that illustrate Wright's book *The Story of the Tower*, was still an undergraduate at the University of Oklahoma at the time, while Harold, Jr. had graduated and started a family. The house that Wright designed for them in Bartlesville, called Hillside, was a long, low structure of the Usonian type with cantilevered balconies. In the course of construction, the young Prices asked for numerous changes in such practical matters as the size of the children's bedrooms, and they were pleasantly surprised that Wright acceded to all of them without any difficulty. Both architect and client were pleased with the result, even though the cantilevered balconies showed a tendency to sag as the years went by — a not infrequent occurrence with Wright's balconies. The problem was addressed by installing steel supports under the low places.

The winter house that Wright designed for the senior Prices in Phoenix was a far cry from their main home in Bartlesville and from the house built for Harold Price, Jr. No longer in the family's possession, it is extremely large and contemporary in design, with a north-facing facade of concrete block whose courses protrude one above the other. This gives the horizontal house a strong vertical thrust at the center, where an open pillared atrium serves as the focal point for living and dining rooms and bedrooms. Some critics of Wright's later work find the house too showy and grandiose, while others applaud its elegance.

ABOVE: *The cantilever balcony takes advantage of the gentle slope of the site.*

OPPOSITE: *A rug designed by Wright is a feature of the long hall of the Price House.*

Robert Llewellyn Wright House,
1953

Bethesda, Maryland

Several years after he designed David Wright's Phoenix residence, Wright undertook the design of a house for his youngest son, Robert Llewellyn Wright, an attorney who practiced in Washington, D.C.

The house was constructed on a wooded slope in Bethesda, Maryland. It is essentially a solar hemicycle, of the kind designed for Herbert and Katherine Jacobs in the mid-1940s, but more elaborate and spacious than the second Jacobs House.

Like most of Wright's Usonian dwellings, the two-story house has a masonry chimney core with a fireplace very similar to that in the David Wright House – a conical shape of concrete block in graduated courses, with a short ledge extending from one side and a semicircular hearth. Concrete block and wood siding were the primary building materials throughout the house, for which Wright also designed the furniture and fittings. The principal rooms open onto a private outdoor area through

glass doors. This was in keeping with the Usonian idea of concrete armatures and glass exteriors, which had dominated Wright's residential designs since the 1930s. The unique feature of this approach was its versatility, which became ever more apparent as such houses sprang up across the country on a wide variety of sites, in climates as diverse as desert and northern prairie. Architect and client could collaborate on a house that utilized many prefabricated and mass-produced elements without compromising individual style, convenience and comfort.

ABOVE: *Lengths of Philippine mahogany were fitted around the hemicyclical facade of the Robert Llewellyn Wright House.*

OPPOSITE: *Wright duplicated the shape of the house in the ottomans and table he designed especially for it.*

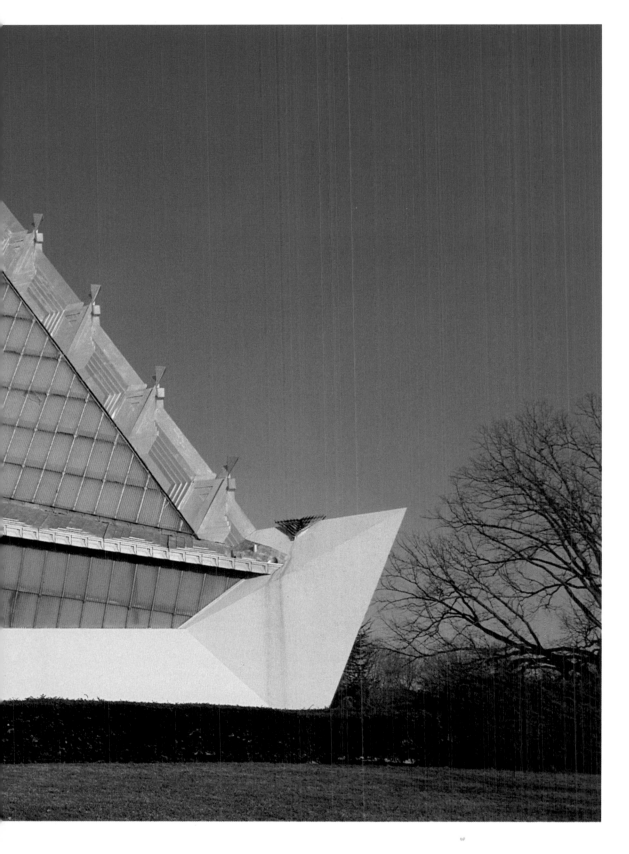

Temple Beth Sholom, 1954

Elkins Park, Pennsylvania

The synagogue commissioned by the congregation of Beth Sholom, under the leadership of Rabbi Mortimer J. Cohen, was one of Wright's most significant achievements. Rabbi Cohen worked closely with the architect from the building's inception, and Wright took up enthusiastically his desire that the temple should be "a mountain of light, a moving Sinai." His response was a great pyramid-like structure of aluminum, steel and glass that rose from an approximately hexagonal concrete base on a tripod formed by steel-and-concrete uprights. A cantilevered canopy overlooks the main entrance.

Inside, a ground-level vestibule leads down toward a chapel and two lounges, one of them connected by a sheltered walkway to the adjacent school and social center. The main auditorium is reached by shallow, curving flights of stairs to the left and right of the entrance. Here a great interior space slopes down gently toward the Ark, faced by a thousand or more seats set in blocks at varying angles and heights. The light coming in from the translucent pyramid overhead changes through the course of the day from silver to gold. At night, the temple radiates light.

The design for this house of worship was derived in part from Wright's unexecuted Steel Cathedral of 1925-26, a visionary project for housing churches and temples of different denominations under one massive tepeelike superstructure of steel and glass. The central mass was to rise over a huge space called "The Hall of the Elements" into which light would pour from above to illuminate the various chapels, cathedrals and temples and their great court. He described the plan as "the devotional church of churches."

ABOVE LEFT: *The translucent glass which is both facade and roof is suspended from a concrete and steel tripod.*

PAGES 170-171: *The concrete tripod removes the necessity of internal support, leaving the interior space entirely open.*

Annunciation Greek Orthodox Church, 1956

Wauwatosa, Wisconsin

In this design for the Milwaukee Hellenic Community, Wright employed abstractions of the primary symbols of the Greek Orthodox faith: the dome and the cross. The ground plan for the church is a Greek cross, and the upper part of the building is carried on arches that support the second level – a bowl-shaped balcony covered by the dome of the roof. The main entrance to the ground level is a broad archway accessed by wide, shallow stone steps with low wings extending from either end that serve as pedestals for gigantic urns. The arch is repeated in the windows that encircle the balcony level, reflecting Wright's interest in Byzantine architecture.

According to Bruce Pfeiffer, director of the Frank Lloyd Wright Archives, who first worked with the architect as an apprentice at Taliesin West: "He often referred to the remarkable domes of the early Byzantine churches, Hagia Sophia in particular. 'The arch was Byzantine,' he wrote, 'and is a sophisticated building act resulting in more sophisticated forms than the lintel of the Mayan, Egyptian, or Greek. Yet it is essentially primitive masonry. Byzantine architecture lived anew by the arch. The arch sprung from the caps of stone posts and found its way into roofing by way of the low, heavy, stone dome. . . . The Byzantine sense of form seems neither East nor West but belongs to both.' " (*Frank Lloyd Wright Drawings*, published in 1990 by Harry N. Abrams, Inc., New York, in association with the Frank Lloyd Wright Foundation and the Phoenix Art Museum).

PAGE 173: *The great dome of the church rests on four piers which form a Greek cross.*

RIGHT: *The gilded dome covers the entire church, not just the center of the transept.*

Picture Credits

© Wayne Andrews/ESTO: 42.

Courtesy of The Art Institute of Chicago: 11 both.

The Bettmann Archive: 7, 10 bottom, 19, 21 bottom, 85, 88 top.

© Judith Bromley: 54, 55, 56 bottom, 58, 59, 74-75.

The Buffalo and Erie County Historical Society: 64, 65.

David Clobes: 110.

The Domino's Pizza Collection: 9 left, 17 top, 18 bottom, 53 bottom, 77 bottom, 88 middle, 89, 95 top.

Ezra Stoller, © ESTO: 8, 21 top, 23, 25 top left and right, 27 top, 86-87, 95 bottom, 120-121, 123, 133, 144, 145, 150 both, 151 both, 154-155.

© 1988 Charlene Faris: 126 both.

Courtesy of Florida Southern College: 134, 135.

Courtesy of The Frank Lloyd Wright Archives: 45, 63 both, 108 both.

Copyright © 1957/The Frank Lloyd Wright Foundation: 14-15.

The Frank Lloyd Wright Home and Studio Foundation: 10 top, 13.

Greenville College: 6 top, 16 bottom, 56 right.

© Pedro E. Guerrero: 112 both, 113 both.

Thomas A. Heinz: 1, 6 bottom, 9 right, 34, 46-47, 47 bottom, 50-51, 57, 61 both, 62 both, 66 bottom right, 66-67, 70-71, 71 both, 78, 79 bottom, 91 bottom, 92-93, 94, 106, 107, 109, 148 both, 157, 158-159, 167, 168-169, 170-171, 174-175.

© Ray F. Hillstrom Jr.: 14 top, 17 bottom, 18 top, 30, 31, 32, 33, 36-37, 38, 40-41, 43, 44, 60, 76, 77 top, 84, 90-91.

Balthazar Korab: 26, 27 bottom, 39, 68-69, 72, 73, 80, 81, 82-83, 88 bottom, 100-101, 103 both, 104, 105, 115, 117, 118, 119, 121 top, 122, 124-125, 128, 129, 137, 138-139, 140 both, 141, 142, 143, 146-147, 149, 152-153, 161, 164-165, 165 bottom, 173.

New England Stock Photo, © Barbara L. Moore: 24; © Alan Detrick: 132.

Courtesy of The Phillips Petroleum Company: 2, 162, 163.

Copyright © 1993 Tom Ploch: 20 both, 96-97, 98 both, 99, 102, 136.

© Ron Schramm: 8-9, 28-29, 48, 52-53, 66 bottom left.

Courtesy of Steelcase, Inc.: 121 bottom.

© Steinkamp/Ballogg Chicago: 12 bottom, 16 top, 35.

UPI/Bettmann Newsphotos: 12 top, 22 both, 25 bottom, 92 top, 111, 127, 166.

© Rudi von Briel: 130-131.

© Western Pennsylvania Conservancy: 114, 116 both.

© 1993 Marco P. Zecchin/Image Center: 156.

Acknowledgments

The author and publisher would like to thank the following people who have helped in the preparation of this book: Elizabeth Montgomery, who did the picture research; Barbara Thrasher, who edited it; and Alan Gooch of Design 23, who designed it.